AF541218

DEVELOPMENT OF CHILD AND HYGIENE

By

Dr. Prakash Chandra Mehta

M.Sc., M.A., Ph.D.

DISCOVERY PUBLISHING HOUSE PVT. LTD.

NEW DELHI-110 002

Published by:
Tilak Wasan

DISCOVERY PUBLISHING HOUSE PVT. LTD.
4383/4B, Ansari Road, Darya Ganj
New Delhi-110 002 (India)
Phone : +91-11-23279245, 43596064-65
Fax : +91-11-23253475
E-mail : parul.wasan@gmail.com
discoverypublishinghouse@gmail.com
web : www.discoverypublishinggroup.com

First Edition: **2013**

ISBN: 978-93-5056-249-9

Development of Child and Hygiene

Printed at:
Dynamic Printers
Delhi

Dedicated to Mother

Smt. Dayawati Mehta W/o Lt. Sh. K.L. Mehta

and KIDS

Saloni, Mitali and Master Somaya

Dedicated to Mother

Smt. Darawati Mehta W/o Lt. Sh. K.L. Mehta

and KIDS

Saloni, Mitali and Master Somaye

Preface

Children are a valuable asset of Nation. There welfare strengthens social and economic development. They have to be protected and well looked after. If a country is to thrive and prosper in all spheres of human activity. The future prospective in the context of the countries development plans ensure a better future, it is very essential for the better care and development plans for the children and special attention should be payed for infants, such sort of schemes should be launched on priority basis.

All over the universe every person or couple or family members like the presence of infants in their family. They pay more attention towards them without any sexual discrimination.

The infants response and sensory capabilities allows him to perceive to react to a vide variety of objects and events. The infants needs other human beings to gratify his dries. The newborn begins life with very few specific emotional and motivational response to others. His experience with human beings during the first two years lays the foundation for his future. The negligence of this period may result in damage to the child's future for development.

In Indian social situation, the children below 4 years or so generally do not get proper attention in respect of their physical and mental development. This tendency is more reflected in rural areas, and specially in the tribal societies. Although in every society, children are the main object of attention and love, but they are ignored and left to natural development of their personality.

Health means some thing more than absence of illness and presence of illness should not necessarily to be taken means poor health. Good Health means the person enjoying physical, emotional, mental and social well being.

The environment factors also affective health of the community and it needs to be handled as an organised activity of the community as a whole. Personal hygiene affects primarily the health of individual and in by and large connected with standard of living. It requires awareness of individuals particular habits which grow by practice and eventually became part of their culture.

In this volume I have discussed the prevailing child rearing practices among the tribals right from inception *i.e.* Prenatal or Neonatal care to infancy alongwith mother *i.e.* pregnant mother care and their dietary pattern and rituals related to infants and their mother. Keeping in view the importance of health in second part, I have discussed the prevailing practices of hygiene *i.e.* sanitation status of the tribals.

This volume is divided in two parts first deals with development of child *i.e.* rearing practices. The first chapter deal with perspectives of child rearing, second chapter reflects the demographic status of Indian Tribes, while third and fourth chapter deals with child development process, Health process and child care. The second part is fully related with Hygiene. Fifth chapter is related to perspectives of Hygiene, while sixth chapter deal with personal Hygiene. The information of this volume is based on fieldwork and personal interviews.

I hope this volume will prove worthwhile in upliftment and betterment of pregnant, lactating mothers and infants. It will also helpful to planners, scholars, voluntary organisations, social scientists and anthropologists to know about the prevailing rearing practices among the Indian Tribes as well as their sanitation practices. I am grateful to all friends who have encouraged me in this onerous task. I indebted to Shri Tilak Vasan of M/s Discovery Publication House, New Delhi for efficient Publication. I am also thankful to my family members—wife Yashoda, daughters Mrs. Sangeeta Nalwaya and Mrs. (Dr.) Sonu Mehta and son Dr. Anurag Mehta for their inspiration and association.

Dr. Prakash Chandra Mehta

Contents

HYGIENE

PANCHSHEEL FOR TRIBAL DEVELOPMENT

- People should develop along the lines of their own genuis and we should avoid imposing anything on them. We should try to encourage in every way their own traditional Art & Culture.
- Tribal rights in land and forests should be respected.
- We should try to train and build up a team of their own people to do the work of administration and development. Some technical personnel from outside will no doubt be needed especially in the beginning but we should avoid introducing too many outsiders into the tribal territory.
- We should not over administer these areas or overwhelm them with a multiplicity of schemes. We should rather work through and not in rivalry to their own social and cultural institutions.
- We should judge results not by statistics or the amount of money spent but by the quality of human character that is evolved.

JAWAHARLAL NEHRU

DEVELOPMENT OF CHILD

1 Perspectives of Child Rearing

Children are a valuable asset of a nation. Their welfare strengthens social and economic development. They have to be protected and well looked after. If a country is to thrive and prosper in all spheres or human activity. The future prospective in the context of the countries development plans ensure a better future, it is very essential for the better care and development plans for the infants and adolescentes, should be launched on priority basis.

The United Nations has declared 1979 as the international year for the child to focus the attention of planners, policy-makers, administrators and social scientists on the various problems encountered by the children, particularly by children in developing countries.

The child situation can be reflected by this fact that in 1978, 120 million children born, cut of which 12 million *i.e.* about 10 per cent of the children should not see their first birth day because of poor health, unhygienic conditions, malnutrition and absence of medical facilities, particularly in the rural areas. As a result, most of the children fails to fails to fulfil social and economic potentialities, which would enable to grow them as useful member of society, this fact perpetuate the cycle of social and economic backwardness among future generations.

During the last four decades a flood of literature has come in the field of trible transformation. The schedule tribes have been given certain safeguards in the constitution. These safe-guards include reservations in parliament and services.

There are a few benefits given to the tribals in the field of education. The objective of these safeguards is to assure fullest participation of the tribals in the economic, political and social life of the country Mainstream. Yet another objective of the safeguards is integrate the tribals in the regional and national Mainstream. The development plans which are implemented among the tribals all over the country are largely sponsored by the Central Government. Among these mention may be made of the trible sub-plan area, Modified Area Development Agencies (MADA) and special projects for primitive groups. The main objectives of these sub-plan are to improve the quality of people so that they may come on part with other nontribal groups who are relatively better off.

In the context of the development and integration of tribals is must be observed that the rearing, and socialization of the infants assume crucial importance. It is useful to see that the development of tribals also takes into consideration, the development of the infants. In fact, the infants are the coming generation who will have to carry forward the legacy of development and integration. Physiologists argue that the formative period for any personality lies some where between 5 to 10 years. According to that the secular democratic and socialistic frame-work, the coming tribal society would be much nearer to the mainstream. Yet another become which the tribals face today is the crisis of cultural identity whereby they strive to retention some of their primordial ethnic traits.

The present enquiry is concerned with the study of child rearing and socializing practices of the Bhils of the tribal - subplan area, the only one of the state of Rajasthan. The Bhils are basically dwellers of hills and forests. Their century long isolation has provided to them a specific identity to child rearing and socializing practices. Every society assures the continuity of its culture through child rearing habits. It is in this context the socializing practices of tribls are very important. Actually, it is the socialization which provides continuity and survival to the community, when we differentiated the tribal society from the nontribal it is the specific ethnicity of the tribals which give differentiation. As a matter of fact the Bhil society has certain primordial ethnic traits which are handed down the coming generation by the process of rearing and socialization.

Children below 4 years or so generally do not proper attention in respect of their physical and mental development. Although in every society children are the object of the affection and love, but they are ignored and left to natural development of their personality and sometimes they are over pampered or literally neglected.

The psychological researches on personality development revealed that the mental development of the child takes place before the age of 3 years therefore, this period is very very important. The parents in general are not aware of this Universal fact, so the child development in most of the societies is at stake. It is observed, that the socialization process vary from society to society variations in behavioural patterns of *Brahmins, Rajputs, Harijans, Minas, Uarasias, Bhils* and other groups are apparent .

The study of the Bhil infants (children) in the age group of 0-4, year is carried out to understand the patterns of child rearing practices in this tribal group, the Bhils are the premitive people who are now coming in close contact with the outside world. Their family and kinship pattern is very compact compared to urban society.

General in Introduction

The plight of the children in India is in no way different from that of children in most developing countries of the world. The child population of India has grown faster than the total population and it shares in the countries population has increased remarkably from over 38 per cent in 1901 to 42 per cent in 1971. The child population aged 0-4, 5-9 and 10-14 years has increased from 29.8 million to 27.6 million, from 32.3 million to 82.0 million and from 28.2 million to 68.6 million respectively during 7 decades *i.e.* from 1901 to 1971. The child population and its percentage to the total population from 1901 to 1971 is given in the Table 1.1.

Table 1.1: Age-wise Distribution of Child Population

(Number)

Census Year	Child population (in thousands) and its percentage in age group			
	0-4	5-9	10-14	0-14
1901 [1]	29,832 (12.56)	32,338 (13.62)	28,196 (11.67)	90.366 (38.05)
1911	34,116 (13.58)	33,861 (13.48)	27,068 (10.78)	95,045 (37.84)
1921	39,920 (12.35)	36.696 (14.65)	29.244 (11.68)	96,860 (38.68)
1931	36,660 (13.18)	38,914 (13.40)	31,469 (11.32)	107,043 (38.50)
1941	42,904 (13.53)	45,291 (14.28)	35,914 (11.33)	124.109 (39.14)
1951	48,085 (13.48)	45,437 (12.74)	43,542 (12.20)	137,064 (38.42)
1961	66,089 (15.06)	54,656 (14.74)	49,287 (11.24)	180,032 (41.04)
1971 [2]	79,560 (14.51)	82,007 (14.96)	68,768 (12.55)	230,335 (42.02)

The Table 1.1 reveals that the lowest growth rate was 1.91 per cent during the decade 1911-1921 and the highest growth rate was 31.25 per cent during the decade, 1951-61.

It may be mentioned here that the proportion of children in most populations is not appreciably effected by migration. The most crucial factor, which determines the proportion of children in any country's population, is the fertility rate of the child-bearing rate. In this connection, Coale writes—"whether a national population is young or old is mainly determined by the member of children women bear. When they bear few, the population is old." He then points out that, in the countries in mortality without counter balancing declines in fertility trend to increase the number of children in the population, and make the population some what younger. This exactly what has happened in india. As a consequence, the share of the child population in the total population has increased significantly.[3]

According to census of 1961 to 1981 the child population in Rajsthan was above 40 per cent of the total population of the state. The age-wise distribution of child population is given as under in the Table 1.2.

The Table 1.2 reveals that in the year 1961 the child population (0-14) was 42.63 per cent, out of which 16.06 per cent were 0-4 age group, 14.95 per cent were 5-9 age group and 11.62 per cent were 10-14 age group. Similarly in the year 1971 and 1981 the child population in the state was 44.17 per cent and 42.44 per cent respectively.

From the Table 1.2 we can say that during 1961 the domination group of child population was 0-4 years having a percentage of 16.06 per cent to the total population of the state . In the year 1981 the dominating group of the age group was 5-9 years having a per cent 14.96 to the total population of the state, while the age group 0-4 years stands second having the percentage 14.07 , while bit less than the age group 5-9 years.

From the above table we can say that in all the age group male child was dominated to female child throughout the four decades. The per cent of male child is bit higher than the female child.

For this study Udaipur district have been selected. This disctrict is also a tribal dominated area and included in the tribal sub-plan area of the state. According to last three decades census *i.e.* from 1961 to 1981 the age-wise child population at Udaipur district is detailed in Table 1.3.

Table 1.2: Age-wise Population of Children

Age group (years)	1961[4]			1971[5]			1981[6]		
	Persons	Males	Females	Persons	Males	Females	Persons	Males	Females
All ages	20,155,602	10,564,082	9,591,520	2,576,806	13,484,383	12,281,423	34,261,862	17,854,154	16,407,708
0-4	3,237,764	1,642,208	1,595,556	N.A.	N.A.	N.A.	4,819,790	2,436,135	2,383,665
5-9	30,13,458	1,578,794	1,434,664	N.A.	N.A.	N.A.	5,126,913	2,673,037	2,453,876
10-14	2,341,123	1,278,502	1,062,621	N.A.	N.A.	N.A.	4,593,951	2,435,513	2,158,438
Total (o-14)	8,592,345	4,499,504	4,092,841	11,381	(thousands)		14,540,654	7,544,685	6,995,969

N.B. In 1971 census the child population was not categorised age-wise.

Table 1.3: Age-wise Population of Children

Age group (years)	1961[7]			1971[8]			1981[9]		
	Persons	Males	Females	Persons	Males	Females	Persons	Males	Females
All ages	1,464,276	755,351	708,925	18,03,542	921,663	881,879	2,356,959	1,191,909	1,165,050
0-4	228,083	114,096	113,987	N.A.	N.A.	N.A.	326,796	161,052	165,744
5-9	225,689	116,862	108,827	N.A.	N.A.	N.A.	353,095	177,811	175,284
10-14	164,234	88,577	75,657	N.A.	N.A.	N.A.	286,955	145,648	141,307
Total (o-14)	618,006	319,535	298,471	N.A.	N.A.	N.A.	966,846	484,511	482,335

N.B. In 1971 census the child population was not categorised age-wise.

The Table 1.3 reveals that in Udaipur district the position of child is similar as in Rajasthan as well as in the country *i.e.* the child population in the district was about 40 per cent throughout the last three decades. In the year 1961, 42.21 per cent were the child population of all the age group (0 14). Out of which 15.58 per cent were 0-4 age group 15.41 per cent were 5-9 age group and 11.22 per cent were 9-14 years age group. Similarly in the year 1971 and 1981 the child population in the district was above 40 per cent the Table 1.3 reveals that from 1961 to 1981 the male child dominate in comparison to female child. In 1981 the female child dominate in the age group of 0-4 years in comparison to famale child. The percentage of male child (0-4) was 6.83, while the females were 7.03 per cent. During 1961 the dominating group of child population was 0-4 years having a percentage 15.58 which is bit lesser than the state percentage.

In the year 1981 the dominating group of the age group was 5-9 years having a percentage 14.98 to the total population of the state, while the age group 0-4 years stands second having the percentage 13.87 which is about one per cent lower than the age group 0-4 years.

Hence, from the above situation, we can say that child plays an very important role in family as well as in society. They are fully dependent or partly dependent on the parents. We can also say that the major part of the children are *i.e.* from the age group 0-9 which is fully dependent on the parents. Specially the infants *i.e.* 0-4 years are totally dependent on the parents and up to this age role of mother is very-very important. We can also say that mother is the builder of the child or she effects the family, society as well as the nation.

The tribal population of India according to 1981 census[10] were 5,16,28, 638 persons (26, 038, 535 males and 25, 590, 103 females) constitute a part of 7.76 per cent (excluding Assam where the census was not held due to unavoidable conditions).

In Rajasthan, the percentage is just double *i.e.* 12.12 per cent of the tribal population during 1981. The details of tribe-wise population of 1961[11], 1971[12] and 1981[13] census given in Table 1.4.

Table 1.4: Tribal Population in Rajasthan

Tribe	1961	1971	1981			%of total S.T.P. Population
			Males	Females	Person	
Rajasthan	2,351,470	3,125,506	2,150,767	2,032,357	4,183,124	100
Bhil, Bhil Garasia, Dholi-Bhil, Dungri-Bhil, Dungri-Garasia, Mewasi-Bhil Rawal Bhil, Tadvi Bhil, Bhagalia, Bhilala, Pawra, Vasava, Vasave	906,705	14,37,937	929,087	911,879	1,840,966	44.01
Bhil-Mina	2,063	17,076	13,766	13,371	27,137	0.65
Damor, Damaria	14,534	14,795	15,937	15,440	31,377	0.75
Dhanka, Tadvi, Tetaria, Vaivi	—	157	7,378	6,733	14,111	0.34
Garasia (Excluding Rajput Garasia)	62,509	52,268	60,225	58,332	118,757	2.84
Kathodi, Katkari, Dhori-Kathodi, Dhorkatkari, Son Kathodi, Son Katkari	—	1	1,236	1,317	2,553	0.06
Kokna, Kokni, Kukna	—	2	91	74	165	Neg. 0.004
Koli Dhor, Tokre Koli, Kolcha, Kolgna	—	166	1,075	1,006	2,081	0.05
Mina	1,155,620	1,532,331	109,1451	995,241	2,086,692	49.88
Naikda, Nayaka, Cholival Nayaka, Kapadia Nayaka, Mota Nayaka, Nana Nayaka	—	32	4,800	4,374	9,174	0.22
Patelia	—	1	931	772	1,703	0.04
Saharia, Sehria, Sahariya	23,299	26,939	20,821	20,124	40,945	0.98
Unspecified	186,740	43,801	3,969	3,494	7,463	0.78

The Table 1.4 reveals that Mina stands first and Bhil stands second while in India Bhil stands third dominate tribal group. Minas are only found in Rajasthan and listed in the scheduled tribe Bhils are inhabitated in Maharashtra, Gujarat, Madhya Pradesh and Rajasthan.

Hence the main consideration is to study the Bhil children, because the high concentration of Bhils in Rajasthan as well as its neighbouring states. In Rajasthan, of Bhils are scattered through out the state. The district-wise distribution of Bhils according to 1981 census[14] is detailed in table 1.5.

Table 1.5: District-wise Tribal and Bhil Population in Rajasthan

Sl.No.	Name of district	All scheduled	Bhil
1	2	3	4
	Rajasthan	4,183,124	1,840,966
1.	Ganganagar	5,095	525
2.	Bikaner	1,496	423
3.	Churu	5,619	82
4.	Jhunjhunu	23,077	94
5.	Alwar	143,858	369
6.	Bharatpur	56,716	514
7.	Sawai-Madhopur	348,130	1,132
8.	Jaipur	380,199	1,668
9.	Sikar	36,652	11
10.	Ajmer	23,183	17,608
11.	Tonk	92,477	7,612
12.	Jaisalmer	10,680	10,532
13.	Jodhpur	28,288	37,559
14.	Nagpur	2,984	221
15.	Pali	69,694	15,069
16.	Barmer	57,038	56,344

1	2	3	4
17.	Jalor	72,361	57,111
18.	Sirohi	125,245	51,420
19.	Bhilwara	121,664	69,113
20.	Udaipur	809,156	392,709
21.	Chittorgarh	223,864	80,687
22.	Dungarpur	440,026	131,871
23.	Banswara	643,866	582,723
24.	Bundi	118,030	23,760
25.	Kota	231,316	49,950
26.	Jhalawar	91,601	51,863

The Table 1.5 reveals that Bhil stands first in Banswara *i.e.* 1.65 per cent and second in Udaipur *i.e.* 21.33 per cent to the total Bhil population of the state. Banswara district is tribal district, where, Udaipur district has mixed population and having seven tehsils where, tribal concentration exists These tehsils are Girwa, Sarada, Salumber, Kotara, Dharayawad, Jhadol and Kherwara.

The rearing practices are different in tribals as compared to the non-tribals. Every tribal group or community have peculiarity of rearing practices as well as social customs and knowledge.

After 1981 census government have restricted the bifurcation of children population. The criteria of population after 1981 census is population up to 0-6 years and above six years. The details of 1991 and 2001 census are given below.

Children in the age group 0–6 and sex ratio : According to 1991 census the children in the age group 0–6 constitute 20.18 per cent of the scheduled tribe population in India as against 17.94 per cent for the total population and 19.63 per cent the Scheduled Caste population. Thus, the Scheduled Tribe population had a relatively higher population of children than the general population as well as Scheduled Caste population. The sex ratio (defined as females per 1000 males) for the Scheduled Tribe population was 972. This is much more favourable to women than the sex ratio among the total poplation (927) or the Scheduled Caste population (922). The details are given in Table 1.6.

Table 1.6: Sex Ratio and Percentage of Population Aged 0-6 for Total Population, Scheduled Caste Population and Scheduled Tribe Population (1991)

Sl. No.	India/State or Union Territory	Sex Ratio (Females per 1000 males)			Percentage of population aged 0-6		
		Total Population	Scheduled Caste Popu-lation	Scheduled Tribe Popu-lation	Total Population	Scheduled Caste Popu-lation	Scheduled Tribe Popu-lation
1	2	3	4	5	6	7	8
	India*	927	922	972	17.94	19.63	20.18
	State						
1.	Andhra Pradesh	972	969	960	16.49	18.02	20.55
2.	Arunachal Pradesh	859	627	998	21.12	19.32	22.02
3.	Assam	923	919	967	19.73	19.67	20.41
4.	Bihar	911	914	971	20.57	22.45	20.12
5.	Goa	967	967	889	11.74	15.28	23.14
6.	Gujarat	934	925	967	16.53	17.32	18.59
7.	Haryana	865	860	–	18.98	21.50	–
8.	Himachal Pradesh	976	967	981	16.25	17.79	17.72
9.	Karnataka	960	962	961	16.63	19.32	18.90
10.	Kerala	1,036	1029	996	13.19	12.90	15.03
11.	Madhya Pradesh	934	944	968	17.11	18.65	20.02
13.	Manipur	958	973	959	16.69	17.07	16.55
14.	Meghalaya	955	821	997	22.18	19.91	23.01

1	2	3	4	5	6	7	8
15.	Mizoram	921	157	982	18.60	8.25	19.12
16.	Nagaland	886	-	946	17.15	-	17.41
17.	Orissa	971	975	1002	16.89	17.91	18.86
18.	Punjab	882	873	-	16.30	18.82	-
19.	Rajasthan	910	899	930	20.13	21.74	21.38
20.	Sikkim	878	939	914	18.37	19.34	17.97
21.	Tamil Nadu	974	978	960	13.33	15.54	16.29
22.	Tripura	945	949	965	18.03	19.64	20.09
23.	Uttar Pradesh	879	877	914	20.27	21.51	20.49
24.	West Bengal	917	931	964	16.98	18.81	19.46
	Union Territories						
1.	Andaman & Nicobar Islands	818	-	947	16.51	-	16.96
2.	Chandigarh	790	810	-	14.92	19.55	-
3.	Dadra & Nagar Haveli	952	925	1022	20.46	15.64	21.87
4.	Daman and Diu	969	1067	931	15.53	17.40	17.62
5.	Delhi	827	834	-	17.06	20.63	-
6.	Lakshadweep	943	-	994	18.30	-	19.14
7.	Pondicherry	979	983	-	13.67	16.23	-

*Excludes figures of Jammu & Kashmir where 1971 census was not taken.

Source: Census of India 1971, sensus-1, Paper-1 of 1993, Union primary census abstract for S.C. and S.T.

Literacy: 29.6 per cent of the Scheduled Tribe population in the age group 7 years and above is found to be literate as per the 1991 census; the literacy rate being 40.65 for males and 18.19 for females. These figures are much lower than the corresponding figures for the total population of India. In fact, these figures are even lower than the corresponding figures for the Scheduled Caste population. If we were to take out the population of North-Eastern states like Nagaland, Mizoram, Meghalaya and Manipur which have a predominantly Scheduled Tribe population and very high literacy rates, the literacy rate of the Scheduled Tribe populaton would be come much lower. That is, the literacy levels among scheduled tribe population in other states are extremely low. In Andhra Pradesh, the literacy rate of the Scheduled Tribe population was just 17.16 per cent. In Rajasthan, it was 19.44 per cent. In case of females, the literacy rates for the Scheduled Tribe population are extremely low; in Rajasthan (4.4), Andhra Pradesh (8.7), Orissa (10.2), Madhya Pradesh (10.7), Bihar (14.8) and Uttar Pradesh (15.0).

According to 2001 census in Rajasthan 0–6 year population was 10,651,002 persons including 5,579,616 male and 5,671,386 female child. The child population comparises 18.51 per cent at the total state population it includes 18.63 per cent male and 18.37 per cent female child.

Concepts

During the last few decades some detailed studies regarding child rearing practices have also been done in U.S.A. and U.K. by several social scientists. They have given many actual facts based on field observations and many scientific studies regarding rearing practices in different groups of societies and races, health and hygiene and the initial behaviour. The infants teaching or behavioral attitude makes a child social and he learns that how he can live and behaves in the society.

1. Socialization

In recent years the term " Socialization" has been widely used by various social scientists, anthropologists, psychilartrists. Psychologists and sociologists. Since " socialization" process has been put to multiple use by specialists from different disciples, it becomes necessary to understand and define the term. Anthropolgists, interested primarily in the study of cultures and folklore, regard socialization as the process by which cultures are transmitted to each new generation, illustrating this point of view, Rutn Benedict says.[15]

" In the last analysis culture exists in the habituated bodies and minds of the people who belong to the culture. Babies are born with undifferentiated responses and children have to conditioned to acquire the habits and characteristics which give individually habits of a community; they must learn the particular habits of a particular culture. By the way in which parents teach their children, in which older children behave toward and punish their pupiles, emotions are selected and cultivated which adopt new generations to the life of their own community."

If we recognise that no development takes place in complete independence of environmental factors, we must accept the fact that the whole process of the development is in a sense the process of socialization. Margaret mead expresses this complete interrelatedness of growth and socialization when she says.[16]

"It is necessary to recognise that the growing child is systematically patterned in every detail, in posture, in tempo as well as in speech, in his way of thinking in his capacity to feel as well as in the forms which his felligs take.

Melville Helskovits has proposed the term 'enculturation' to signify the process of 'socialization'. In fact, both refer to the process of growing into culture, becoming the kind of creature encouraged by it, 'taking' the culture as a part the self.

"At the time of birth, the human infant is unable to take part in any human society. It has no conception of a 'self' on its own. It is unable to distinguish between its own inner life and the 'reality' of objects independently existing. It has no idea that such a distinction is possible. Gradually human infants develop into an adequate member of human societies. This gradual development is largely a process of learning. Socialization is, therefore, learning, that enables the learner to perform social roles. Thus, not all learning is socialization, since some learning is irrelevant to motivation and ability, necessary for participation in social systems. Culture is what is learned in socialization."[17]

Socialization must be distinguished from that growing up and gradual changing of the organism which we call maturation, and which is inevitable provided that the organism survives without serious physical injury. All learning involves some change in the organism. The process of socialization and maturation proceed together in the early years of the life, and the attempts to teach, while have varying effects depending upon the point reached in the maturation of the child.[18]

"Timing is an important factor in the process of socialization. It is foolish to expect the child to be quiet he is capable of sustained inhibition. Since the infant at birth is largely helpless, he is dependent upon adults for his survival and for training. Moreover, the process by which adults train him is not left to their unguided ingenuity. On the contrary, ways of training children are part of the culture of every society, and the task is performed by occupants of definite roles. The family in particular is organised in such a way as to make socialization possible."

A growing body of knowledge derived largely from the work of cultural anthropologists indicates that human relationships can be patterned in an almost infinite number of ways. Cultural anthropologists have focussed their attention on behaviours which in the past have been considered "instinctive", that is, necessary and immutable. They have studied intensively such matters as behaviour associated with masculinity and femininity, and with child rearing.

They have examined the manifestation of aggression and hostility, the operation of competition and cooperation. From their findings, it has become increasingly evident that none of those behaviours was instinctive on the other hand, they were all learned behabiour which was regarded by the group as the only "correct" and admissible one.[19]

It is important for the child to have the love and affection which is necessary for his proper development socially as well as emotionally, the attitude of the mother towards her pregnancy and the sesonsibilities of motherhood is a first consideration. This will depend in large part on her past experiences, and the goals which she has set for marriage and motherhood. Where the closely linked emotional and social needs of the mother have not been met adequately, she finds it difficult to accept the role of motherhood and to meet the child's need for the social development. The mother's ability, also for easy social relations, as well as to be relaxed and secure in her handling of the child, will affect her role as a handling of the child, will affect her role as a mother not only in caring for the infant but for the family as a whole.[20]

2. Prenatal (Neonatal) care and maternal health

Modern pregnancy care takes a full view of the family and sees its needs in a broad concept of the physical, emotional, and social environments in which its members live. The physical requirements of the mother to be, as a pregnant obstetrics can offer, and rightly so, for the first goal of pregnancy care is the safety of the mother and her baby in his great event. But "safe delivery" implies more. For the mother this is a chance to play her part in the development of her family unhampered by any injuries of child birth and emotionally able to meet her increased problems. For the baby it is the right to be born well, uninjured, and with his potential developing a useful life.[21]

Safety takes precedence over all case in pregnancy and continues well beyond the child bearing period. It is far better to prevent rickets in the child than to do a caesarean in the adult for a deformed pelvis. Premarital and preconceptual examinations, including a careful history, give warming of abnormalities that may exist, and permit corrective measures. The interval between pregnancies offers another opportunity for repair of physical deficiencies that may have arisen during the previous confinement.[22]

The normal course of development as set by them can be altered by changes in the environment of the fetus in the uterus. Some contributing factors may be maternal dietary inadequacies, viral infections as for example, german measles during the first, six to ten weeks of pregnancy. A child whose mother has had german measles in early pregnancy may have congenital defects. The virus evidently affects the young developing tissues of the brain eyes, ears of heart. Such malformations, however, are rase. Among women who smoke cigarettes during pregnancy, there is a tendency to have babies of premature deliveries (surgeon general's committee on smoking and health: Report. U.S. Public Health Service, 1962.[23]

Maternal health during pregnancy is also important, passamanick, Lilienfied and Co-workers (1954) have found and association between the frequency of abnormalities of prenatal and immediately postnatal periods and the frequency of abnormalities of prenatal and immediately postnatal periods and the frequency of cerebral palsy, epilepsy, mental deficiency, reading disorders, and behaviour disorders reported by teachers.[24]

Asian flu during pregnancy has been found to increase the number of infantile anomalies, the incidence of anomalies was higher when the disease occurred during the first three months of pregnancy. Asian flu also increased the number of premature births as well as the still birth rate and prenatal mortalities.[25]

The term 'infancy' derived from the latin, infantia, which means an inability to speak so, strictly speaking, infency refers to the period of development from birth to the time when a baby begins to tack, usually during the second year of life. Some professionals have is that they consider infancy almost entirely as a period of preparation for later life, this can be considered up to the age of 4th years. Infancy is an important time in itself for babies and their parents.

For parents infancy is a time of many varied emotions of joy, love, fulfilment as well as frustration, anger and all too often, exhaustion.

We measure a life span—our age from the moment of birth, which we see conventionally as our beginning. But of course most babies are already about 40 weeks old when they take birth, and have passes through many physical changes in the womb of the mother. This early life 90 is in the form of expections and birth of a baby end it.

At birth the baby undergoes a sudden change in environment and has to make a every rapid transition from fetal life in which all food and oxygen arrive via the umblicial cord from the mother to that of a creature that is air beathing and must digest its own food. The first big shift is in the patterns of circulation, when the blood flow changes so that it passes through the lungs. At some time, breathing moments begin and air passes in and out of the lungs. The period quiet alertness after birth, may represent a kind of recovery period from this first transition. New borns do nourished in pregnancy.[26]

3. Birth of Child and Rearing

The birth of a child is a crucial moment having high risk for both mother and child. In the urban areas delivery is performed in hospitals/dispensaries/Nursing homes by the trained nurses and Doctors. But in the rural area non-availability of medical services, delivery is performed by trained professional *Dai*.

In tribal society the delivery is performed generally by the old women of family. In tribal society the delivery or child birth takes place in different ways. Some of them are very interesting the detail's of procedures and birth ceremonies performed in few prominant tribes are as under:

Among the *Uralis* in south India, when a women is about to become a mother, she goes to a tree-house far away from the habitation. She is not even assisted by women in her delivery, except from a distance. Pollution in their case lasts 21 days and on the twenty-second day she takes bath. During the period the father of the newly the *Navadis* except that she is assisted by a woman.[27]

As regards birth ceremonies, those of *Badagas* are simple. The ceremony is performed in the seventh month of a woman's first pregnancy. This is called *Kanni Kattodu* or Kanni Kaakodu. The delivery takes place in the verandah of the house which is temporarily converted into a room. Afterwards the woman is removed to the other apartment, and she has to hold the reascent moon before her impurity can be removed. After a month, the mother returns to the house of her husband. The naming of the child occurs on the seventh, ninth or eleventh day. The shaving ceremony is held when the child is seven month old.[28]

The *Chenenchus*[29] have a brief ceremonals, on the birth of the child. This is thus as a child is born, the umbilical cord is cut with knife or arrow, and the child is washed in cold or hot water according to the season. On the forth day an old woman gives a name to the child.

Like the Badagas, the *Kallans,*[30] too observe a pollution period, when a child is born. The naming ceremony is held on the seventh day after the birth. The ear-boring ceremony precedes this.

Among the *Koravas*[31] it is believed that delivery of a pregnant woman is accelerated by the mid-wife putting a pinch of earth into the woman's mouth. The mother is held to be unclean ten days after the delivery. The name of the child is given nine days after birth.

Among the *Kotas*[32] when a woman is pregnant, for the first time, her husband lets his hair grow long and leaves his finger nails uncut. The expectant mother is removed to a hut after delivery. This hut is particularly month for the women in the circumstances. In the first confinement, a mother has to spend three months in this hut. As regards the actual delivery, the birth do not provide much assistance to the mother.

The *Munds*[33] conceive of the birth of a child as the result of the union between a man and a woman. There is no maked preference for a male-child, though it is expected that a higher value be places upon a male issue in a patriarchal society. They believe that it is only through a some that a generation might continue. There is no special restriction on food and work for the expectant mother. She continues to carry on her house hold duties as long as her health permits. As soon as the pain starts the expectant mother is taken to the specially prepared hut. During the delivery older women assist in the birth of the child. Usually no medicine is applied for difficult delivery, but massaging the abdomen with oil and turmeric powder may be resorted to. After the child is born the umbilicial cord is cut with a knife and the naval cord is tied with a piece of unbleached cotton string. The placenta is buried in the ground within the domicilement soon for eight days. In mundas pollution period of eight days is observed. The rituals if naming the child also takes place on the nineth day.

When the mother is at work she carries the baby on her bact, securely bundled. This is common among the tribes like Munda, Oran, Santhal and practically all the tribes of middle India.

Among the *Gonds* of Chhattisgarh a woman is supposed to keep away from a horses shadow to prevent an unduly larger period of pregnancy. They believe, the woman would have to carry her pregnancy for a year just as a more does. During pregnancy some ritual prescription and taboos put not only a check on her free movement but also control the behaviour of her husband. Among the gonds delivery normally takes place in a specially built hut. Just after the birth the baby is placed on a winnowing fan full of grain and then kept aside for the future use. Pollution period is observed for 40 day. Naming ceremony is observed on 41th day after the delivery.[34]

In *Santhals,*[35] primary case of the new born baby is being taken by mid-wife or any other near relative who acts during delivery. The process includes after detaching the umblicial cord. Breast feeding is the main food for the infants. No other suitable diet has been introduced to the baby until he is 7 or 8 months old. There are certain beliefs among them which prohibit them to the use of other animals mild for the rearing of the infants. Cow's milk is generally avoided as they believe that it is too heavy, and it cause indigestion to the infants. In normal course, the child is breast fed for a long time until a subsequent on is born. Mothers do not feed the babies spontaneously. They fed the babies when they cry for it there by indicating hunger. The main problem among the santhal children is malnutrition. Though poverty and ignorant are the main reasons for malnutrition.

J.K. Doshi (1975), for instance has worked extensively in the *'pai'* village of Udaipur district. He has an anthropological bias. He describes the cutting of naval—cord and narrates the rituals associated with it. He also, writes about the different stages of development of a Bhil child along with the ritual practices.

T.B. Naik (1962) and S.L. Doshi (1978) have vividly described the details about family and family practices regarding child development. Actually these Authors have tried their best to give an ethnographic portrait of the socialization of Bhil infants.

4. Nutrition

The proper feeding of infants is very important, the infant should be encouraged to establish a feeding regime which will satisfy the hunger and avoid frustration, and this is turn should lead to healthy appetive throughout childhood. The diet of the infant or child should be adequate in total calories, fluid content, and bulk, and should cover the minimum nutritional requirements of the infact in essential constituents.

Improved nutrition has certainly responsible for the acceleration of growth and maturation. In deficiency in feeding causes many infections and diseases, it may also causes deaths of the infacts. In developing countries malnutrition is very much common.

The digestive tract of the infant differs in several respects from that of the older child, and its capacity is correspondingly limited. The absence of teeth excludes the chewing of solid food, and although saliva is excreted at birth, salivary digestion in early infancy is negligible. Liquid food in the form of milk is normally obtained by sucking, a reflex act at first consisting of regular and co-ordinated moment of jaws and controlled by a centre in the medulla. The reflex begins to disappear in the later part of the first year.

The stomach at birth and during infancy lies with its long axis placed transversely, and only gradually reaches the adult from and position at the age of about eleven years. Its capacity and shape are extremely variable depending not only on food but also depends on air-swallowing .

(A) Breast-Feeding

Breast-milk is a very complicated mixture of fats, proteins, sugars, minerals and water that can provide all the food required by a baby for the infancy period. The formation of breast milk is controlled by a number of harmones, principally prolactin. These co-ordinate the development of breasts with the growth of the lfetus through pregnancy and ensure that colostrum is available at birth.

Psychologically breast feeding enables the mother to achieve feedings of warmth and protectiveness thereby enhancing her self-esteem as a mother for the infant, breast milk is nutritionally adequate and balanced, safe and hygienic, and provides immunity against gastro-intestinal and respiratory infactions and allergies.[36]

It was observed that the incidence of infections, expecially major ones such as diarrhoes and septicaemia were significantly lower in the groups which received human milk.[37]

The composition of breastmilk varies from first few days when colostrum is produced, through a transitional phase of 2-3 weeks, leading to the production of mature milk. Colostrum is secreted in small amounts upto 40 ml and has a different composition compared with the mature milk containing less band C vitamins, fat and lactose, but more protein, minerals and A, D, E and K vitamins. It also contains antibodies which help to protect the infact against infection. Breastmilk is the ideal food for infants because its composition is exactly what the child requires and can digest breast-feeding also has a contraceptive effect on the mother.[38]

If the babies are placed directly on to the breast after birth, it is possible that infant infection and consequent malnutrition could be reduced substantially.[39]

This is still the ideal method of infant feeding not withstanding the great improvements in artificial feeding of the last fifty years. Breast feeding should therefore be encouraged unless there is some real contradiction. The familiar agreements in its favour still hold good. Human breast milk is the food most perfectly adopted to the infant's needs, it is provided at the optimum temperature and the risk of contamination is minimal. It has the economic advantage of passing direct upsets is significantly less in breast fed infants as compared with those artificially fed except under optimal hygienic conditions. The comfort enjoyed by the infant in contact with the soft breast instead of hard bottle and the confidence gained by the mother in supplying the infant's needs herself, are factors in the successful rearing of infants which it is difficult to assess statistically. But which may be assumed to have importance.[40]

The preparation of the mother for breast feeding and her success in breast feeding have two important aspects which may be referred to as psychological and physiological. Both are of sufficient importance to receive attention regularly as a part of prenatal and post partum care until the infact is weared. The essential aspects of the psychological preparation are to be sure that the mother understands what is involved for herself and her infant of the breast, colostrum, is well recognized. It contains more total protein and has a higher proportion of euglobulin, the serum protein concerned with immunity, than does later breast milk.[41]

Breast milk is perfect food for a baby. It has the right amount of body-building protein that the body needs so that he can grow. It has much energy-giving corbohydrate and fat, as well as all vitamins, minerals and water that the baby needs. Breast milk is safe and has none of the micro-organisms (germs) that are so often found in dirty feeding bottles. Breast milk does not ever go bad - even when a mother is pregnant. It is not ever hot or cold, it is perfectly warm all the time. The milk that comes from a mother,s breast in the first day after the child birth is thin and watery and is named colostrum. Because it is very good for babies, they should be put to their mother's breast as soon as they are born.[42]

Breast feeding only is enough for the six months of a child's life, and there is not usually any need to give him water or other drinks. (When he has diarrhoea, he may need other liquids) when a baby is hot and needs to drink something, it is good idea to let him first get as much as he wants and can find in the breasts.[43]

In aborigionals and in primitive groups, breast feeding is very much popular. The mothers fed their infants for a long period which varies from $1^{1/2}$ year to $2^{1/2}$ years of age. The other benefit of the breast feeding is that it reduces fertility *i.e.* during the breast feeding is also helpful in family planning measure.

(B) Supplementary Food

Initially the infant is fed with the breast feeding but sometimes in early period they could not satisfied by the mothers milk at that time it is necessary to give some alternate food, like animal milk and other milk products. Semi-liquid and solid food products. After the age of 6 months generally infant feel hunger and not feed properly by the breast feeding, in other words we can say that after time passes the quantity of breast milk reduces and infant could not fed properly or the hunger of the infant increases as he grows. So supplementation is necessary for proper feeding.

Supplementary food differs from person to person. Those families who are well to do give good quality of food products like bottle feeding from powder milk, canned packed baby food, fruit juices and other solid and semi-solid food products. But in the rural areas or the in medical class and poor people who can not afford costly food products, fed their infants by their regular food which they take.[44]

On the contrary, feeding a child commercial milk can put it at a nutritional disadvantage milk powders are expensive, required to be made up to the correct concentration for each feed which clean boiled water and given using clean utensils. This is not always possible. Although breast milk in an excellent source of nutrition beyond 4-6 months of age, just as it is the ideal food during this period, it is not sufficient to satisfy all the children requirements. It needs to be supplemented with other foods. This can be adequately done using local foods such as rice, lentils and vegetables and does not require expensive pre-prepared foods. The main nutritious, non - milk foods are pulses and cereals which may be introduced from 6 months onwards. In general, supplementation began late and had poor nutritional value which may be cause of the decline in nutritional status from 6 month onwards.[45]

The very early introduction of soft solid foods, drinks ice-cream, vitamin preparations, etc. Through all available mass-media, require much more critical evaluation in terms of child health and fitness in adult life than they commonly receive.

The excessive use of refined sugar is not only a nutritional hazard, but it also an important factor in producing dental caries. While the elimination of disease due to nutritional deficiency from infant and childhood communities is wholly desirable. It may reasonably be assumed that there is an optimum nutritional status which is not advantageous to exceed.[46]

A complementary feed is an artificial feed given immediately after a breast feed when the breast-milk supply is inadequate for the infants requirement. A supplementary feed is an artificial feed completely replacing one of the breast feeds, complementary feeding should be looked on as a temporary measure designated to tide over a period of deficient lactation *e.g.* when lactation is established late or when the mother is temporarily over tired or debilitated.

The period between one and two years of age as far as nutritional needs are concerned is a transitions period. During the transitional period of late infancy the child learns to feed himself and usually gives up his bottle if he has not done so earlier. He learns to eat a wider variety of foods in kinds and consistency. Since this is a period when life time habits are being established, the handling of the child in this transitional period is of important as it was in early infancy. Failure to respect his natural appetite, his individual day to day preferences, his desire to feed himself, and his need to become acquainted with new food and foods of different consistency may result in feeding problems.[47]

Studies have shown that improvement of inadequate diets can improve the health and growth of children. Spies and his co-workers (1949) have demonstrated to inadequate diets of malnourished children will improve their growth. But the supplement very few of the children completely reduced their growth lag. This was thought to be due, separately or in various combinations, to too little additional food, too little time on the experimental diet, imbalances in the diet and irreversible changes produced by long-term under-nutrition. In India a multipurpose food composed of groudnut flour and bengalgram flour fortified with calcium phosphate, thiamine, ribosavin Vitamins A and D, which provides protein, minerals and vitamins, is being used to supplement inadequate diets of children.[48]

A mother's breast milk usually given a child all the food he needs till he is about six months old. But when he is six months old, he has become so big that breast milk is not enough by itself and his mother should start to give him porridge. If a child is to go on growing well, he must eat parridge as well as breast milk, before he is 7 month old. Some mothers do not give a child his first porridge once a day when he is most hungery. When he is eating it well, he can have it 2 or 3 times.[49]

5. Weaning

Weaning also plays an important role in child health and nutrition. There has no earmarked time for the weaning. Weaning period from family to family. In educated mass and in urban areas weaning is started after 6 month age of the infant, in rural areas and in primitive groups weaning is generally started after the age of $1^1/_2$ years.

The length of time that breast feeding should be continued will depend to some extent on the condition of the mother, but from the point of view of the baby it is usually found in practice that it is considerably easier to start weaning at six months. When the baby is showing new interests in putting outside objects into his mouth, then if it is left to nine or tenmonths. From the nutritional point of view, it should be remembered that there is no harm in the baby having drinks of breast-milk through out the second year, milk is inadequate as the sole source of iron after three to four months and there is a real danger of nutritional anaemia occurring if breast feeding is continued too long without supplementing with iron-continuing foods. Weaning should not be begun if the baby is ill or during very hot weather, for the normal infant a practical policy is to omit one breast each week during the seventh month, until the baby is off the breast early in the eight month. At this age the baby can digest whole cow milk and solids. The reaction to a new taste is often a negative one, and the baby should be offered new foods, with a chance of indulging preferences rather than being forced to eat them.[50]

Some valuable studies on self-elected diets during todleer period have been carried out by Davis (1928) and others, in which infants of the weaning age were allowed to eat what they choose out of a reasonably large selection of foods. It was found that they not only throve on this regime, but the diets they selected were adequate in quantity and practically optimal in composition.

During weaning period artificial feeding or supplementary food is given to the infants. Generally Animal milk is initially given to infant. In animal milk, cow milk is mostly preferred in comparison to other milk, because it is very much similar or nearer in composition to the human milk. It is also early digestible to the infants. Generally the milk is diluted maximum up to 50 per cent. In India where cows are rare or not easily available goat or other animal milk is given to the infants, but in few part of the country people prefer goats milk in comparison to cow's milk.

Practically all the standard methods of artificial feeding of infants are based on the use of cow's milk, and since the digestive system of the young infant is perfectly adapted to the digestion of human milk , some modification of the lotier is advisable. If the composition of human and cow's milk is compared, it is seen that human milk have higher carbohydrates. The all proportions are detailed as under in Table 1.6.

Table 1.6: Composition of Human and Cow Milk

Sl.No.	Particular	Human milk	Cow' s milk
1.	Caloric value (per 100 ml)	70	70
2.	Carbohydrate (Lactose) Per cent	7	4.75
3.	Fat	3.5-4	3.5-4
4.	Protein	1.25	3.4
5.	Lactalbumin	0.75	0.4
6.	Caselnogen	0.5	3.0
7.	Minerals	0.2	0.73

In other words we can say that cow's milk in some form is the principal ingredient in almost all feeding mixtures. During weaning period powder milk or other baby foods are used. They are generally prepared by the cow milk. Hence during weaning human milk is replaced by cow milk and its products.

This is also a very important period for child when he starts regular food after weaning. It also effects the child health as well as nutritional habits. Initially infant requires his own special plate, it is not given or proper attention is not paid on his diet the child will be suffer by malnutrition and got sick. So keeping in view the requirement of the child the regular food is to given according to the taste of the child and slowly the eacting habits should be moulded according the parents desire. The breast feeding should not stopped suddenly, but it should be stapped gradually.

A childs physical habits will strengthen or impair his appetite and thus his interest in and attitude towards food. Regularity and the spacing of meals, satisfactory elimination, plenty of exercise, fresh air and sunshine and enough sleep and rest to permit recuperation from the activities. There is much truth in the saying " too tired to eat". The tired child, whether he is tired from vigorous exercise or from the other many causes of fatigue, is not ready for his needs. A balance diet is also important.[52]

In his early years the child spends most of his time at home and it is at home that he requires his eating habits. Parents, in planning for their children, can prepare for them by taking stock of their own food patterns and setting the family eating habits in readiness for the children. This is important form even before the child has moved from infancy into early childhood, he begins to acquire the tastes of his family for the particular foods and food combinations they prefer. The parent's attitudes toward their children's eating are extremely important. According to Baldwin' s study (1945). Food appetite was found in homes in which strict disciplinary methods were combined with approval of the child.[53]

The food eaten and attitudes toward food vary from one culture to another. In other words to understand children's eating habits, to know the cultural background of the family that dictates the values of foods and the uses of food in daily living, such as acceptable or unacceptable foods, taken on special occasions, foods associated with religious practices, patterns of meals, eating behaviour and the manner in which the children learn about food. The economic condition also effect the food stuff and reacting habits.

Every child at birth has the basis for establishing good eating habits, namely, the hunger drive. The gratification from taking food at the time hunger sensations occur is the beginning of establishing good eating habits. With this experience as a beginning, the child changes his eating behaviour with increasing maturation and experience. From the early weeks of life taste discrimination is present and provides a basis for the development of selective appetite or the liking and disliking of foods. These differences with age and between individuals of the some age may be responsible in part for individual children's differences in accepting foods.[54]

The balance diet proposed by I.C.M.R in 1981 are detailled as under in the Table 1.7.

Table 1.7: Proposed Balance Diet by I.C.M.R.

Sl.No.	Name of Food	Age Group (In years)	
		1-3	4-6
1.	Cereals	175 (Gram)	270 (Gram)
2.	Pulses	35	35
3.	Leafey Vegetables	40	50
4.	Root Vegetables	10	20
5.	Other Vegetables	20	30
6.	Milk	300	250
7.	Oil and Fat	15	25
8.	Sugar and Gur	30	40

Similarly the I.C.M.R. in 1981 has proposed essential requirements in the balance diet from infancy to adolescent are detailed in Table 1.8.

Hence the infants should be given balance diet and it must have all the essential components. If decay in any component the infant will suffer from deficiency diseases. In other words we can also say that child will be malnutriated. In developing country where economic constraints exists, malnutrition can be seen very often.

6. Health

Health is directly related term to the development of young children. Particularly because the age group of 4 years or say infants, because infants have very low resistance power and comes in grip of diseases/infections very easily. Growth is the most sensitive and practical measure of good health and development. Strategies which accept mild or malnutrition prior to effective intervention should be reoriented to emphasize early detection of growth.

The most common infections in children in Dharavi (Bombay-sleem) are gastroenteritis, respiratory tract infections and worm infections. Skin infections are also common but probably have less impact on the child' s nutrition status. Each infection decreases the child's appetite, burns up energy stores and in the case of gastroenteritis. Leaves the child dehydrate. Thus the child with few reserves becomes nutritionally depleted, more prone to further infection and enters a process of decline from which it may not recover. Loss of weight and the slowing of growth reflect this. The lack of colostrum and hence antibodies at this critical time may be an important factor in the childs susceptibility to infection. Animal milk, is not boiled immediately before feeding the child is a rich source of dangerous organisms especially if diluted with unclean water.[55]

The combined effect of poor medical facilities in rural areas, poor nutrition, unhygienic conditions of living and high

Table 1.8: Proposed Essential Diet by I.C.M.R. for Children (Infancy to Adolescent)

Age Group		Net calories (k.cal)	Protin (gram)	Calcium (gram)	Iron (Ml.Gm)	Vitamin -A		Thyamin (Ml.Gm)	Ribo-flavin (Ml.Gm)	Nicotinic Acid (Ml.Gm)	Vitamin B6 (Ml.Gm)	Escarbic Acid (Ml.Gm)	Folic Acid (kg)	Vitamin B-12 (kg)	Vitamin (I.U.)
						Ratinol	B-Kerotin								
0-6 month		1.18kg	2.0 kg	0.5-0.6	1.0 MG/kg.	400	–	55 kg.	71 kg.	780 kg.	0.3	20	25	0.2	
6-12 month		108kg	1.7 kg			300	1200	54 kg	65 kg	710	0.4				
1-3 year		1220	22.0			250	1000	0.6	0.7	8	0.6				
4-6 year		1720	29.4	0.4-0.5	20-25	300	1200	0.9	1.0	11	0.9				
7-9 year		2050	35.6			400	1600	1.0	1.2	14	1.2			0.2-1.0	
10-12 year	Boys	2420	42.5			600	2400	1.2	1.5	16	1.6				200
	Girl	2260	42.1					1.1	1.4	15	1.6	40			
13-15 years	Boys	2260	51.7	0.6-0.7	25	750	3000	1.3	1.6	18	2.0				
	Girl	2360	43.3		35			1.2	1.4	15	2.0				
16-18 years	Boys	2820	53.1	0.5-0.6	25	750	3000	1.4	1.7	19	2.0				
	Girl	2200	44.0		35			1.1	1.3	15	2.0				

fertility are part of the reality behind these figures. The heavy burden of repeated births of Indian women is extensively documented. Apart from it being a contributory factor in itself to high maternity mortality, its effect as a drain on the nutritional status and energy on women is obvious. According to the committee on the status of women (Towards Equality, 1975) in over a third of the districts of India, women's average age at marriage is below that an Indian women spends on an average 194 months of her life in pregnancy and lactation. Poor maternal nutrition and health, apart from it effect on the mother's survival, also determines the survival chances of the infant.[56]

According to the Indian Council for Medical Research (studies on pre-school children. 1972), in a large sample of male and female pre-school children, at all ages between I and 5 years boys tended to be Faller and heavier than girls. The nutritional standard of boys, gauged by arm circumference was also better than that of girls. The selected nutritional status indicators for boys and girls recommended by the I.C.M.R. is detailed below for a healthery infant[57] in Table 1.9.

Table 1.9: Standard Health Norms Recommended by I.C.M.R.

Age group (years)	Height (cms)		Weight (Kgs)		Armcircum-ference	
	M	F	M	F	M	F
1-1½	70.8	69.3	7.8	7.3	12.5	12.1
1½-2	74.2	73.3	8.5	8.0	12.7	12.5
2-2½	78.2	77.1	9.4	9.0	13.0	12.8
2½-3	81.8	80.0	9.8	9.7	13.0	13.0
3-4	86.2	84.9	11.1	10.7	13.4	13.4
4-5	93.9	92.6	13.2	12.6	14.0	13.9

Health means something more than the absence of illness and the presence of illness should not necessarily be taken to man poor health. There are children who really have a definite illness, but equally rerely can be said to be in good health in the sense of enjoying physical, emotional, mental and social well being.

Some of the factors which really constitute health are the resistance of the child has when exposed to infections agents, his ability to make successful adaptations to disease or stress of other sorts, and in some measure his "learning" or ability to improve his defense mechanisms through illness experiences. In appraising a child's total health one must take into account his susceptities to illness and more particularly how readily he recovers from illness and how satisfactorily he keeps on growing and developing without important as a result of them. Any illness may be accompanied by loss of appetite, poor intake and poor utilization of food, while febrile illnesses increases caloric, fluid other specific needs. Failure to absorts or actual loss of nitrogen during illness in common. Severe, chronic, or recurrent acute illness are likely too have deleterious effects of some type or degree on physical growth or on emotional, mental, or social development.[58]

The severty of infectious diseases has been shown to vary with age. In infancy they are relatively severe, due to a large measure to the immaturity of physiological processes *e.g.* Tuberculosis. There are various means of stimulating immurity to certain specific infectious diseases, in some producing almost lifelong immunity, while in others obtaining varying degrees of immunity.

In the latter prevention can be improved with occasional small repeat immunizations or booster inoculations *e.g.* D.P.T.. and polio vaccine which are given from infant in three doses after a interval of every month, fourth dose is given after 5 years, while B.C.G., small pox immunization are given once in the life. These vaccines are prepared from cultures of the bacteria or viruses causing the diseases which they are designed to prevent. There are two general types. Killed vaccines and living but attenuated vaccines. Killed viruses require two or usually three injections to stimulate the organism for antibody production. Living vaccines may be used if they have been sufficiently altered or attenuated so that they can no longer produce the typical diseases, but still can induce immunity to it. In other words we can say that immunisation vaccinations in infancy reduces the severity of infections and mortality.

The current immunization programmes carried out almost routinely throughout all the states of the country. This programme is launched by the govt. of India and other agencies include vaccination against smallpox, immunization against diphtherias, Tetanus and pertussis (whooping cough) known as D.P.T., Polio vaccine and B.C.G. The mats immunization programme is boon for the infants and it has reduced the infant mortality, disorders and handicaptedness.

Hence during the infancy nutrition is important, while health precautions can not be avoided. In other words we can say that in infancy nutrition is directly related with health. In infancy the child care is very important and negligence can convert into total incidence.

Why this Study

(*i*) This study will be helpful in knowing the child rearing practices among the Bhils.

(*ii*) This will be useful in implementing various child welfare programmes including I.C.D.S and also helping in assessing the impact of I.C.D.S. on Bhil society.

(*iii*) It will also helpful to educate young mothers during pregnancy and improvement of traditional - Nutrition system by this way infant mortality will be reduced.

(*iv*) It will highlight the importance of the infant in society as well as in family and importance in future development.

Area of Study

Out of 7 tehsils of Udaipur district, one tehsil is selected for the field work and two villages have been selected from this tehsil. The selection criteria of the village is one village should be nearer to the tehsil and other will be remote village.

Hence, for the study Girwa tehsil has been selected and have the all means of communication and the head quarter of the tehsil is situated in Udaipur city. So in this study we can also assess the impact of urbanisation on the tribal culture.

From Girwa tehsil, two villages, Dheekli and Lakarwas have been selected for the field work.

REFERENCES

1. Mukherjee, S.B. *The Age Distribution of the Indian Population*, A reconstruction for the states and territories 1881-1961 (cttonolulu. East-West Population Institute, 1976), P. 65 for 1901 to 1961 child population.
2. Census of India 1971, *Social and Cultural Tables*, series 1, Part II-C (ii), P. 199.
3. Ed. Srinivasan, K., Saxena, P.C. and Kanitker Tara: *Demographic and Socio - Economic Aspects of the Child in India*, 1979, Himalaya Publishing House, Bombay, p. 33.
4. *Census of India, 1961*, Vol. XIV, part II-C (1) Social and Cultural Tables, Rajasthan, p. 85.
5. *Census of India, 1971, Social and Cultural Tables*, Series-I Part II-c (ii) , pp. 199-211 and Atlas of the Child in India by Moonispal Raja, & Sudesh Nangia 1986, Concept Publishing Company, New Delhi, pp. 304-307.
6. Census of India, 1981, *Social and Cultural Tables*, Part-IV A, Rajasthan, p. 86.
7. Census of India, 1961, Vol. XIV, part I-C (i) Social and Cultural Tables, Rajasthan, p. 93
8. Census of India, 1971, *Social and Cultural Tables*, Series-I, Part II-C (ii), pp 199-211 and Atlas of the Child in India by Moonis Raza & Sudesh Nangia 1986, pp 304-307. Concept Publishing Company, New Delhi.
9. Census of India, 1981, *Social and Cultural Tables*, part IV-A Rajasthan, p. 126.

10. Census of India 1981, Series-I Part II-B (iii) Primary Census Abstract (Scheduled tribes), pop. XIX-XXI and 4-15.

11. Census of India, 1961, Vol. I, India part V-A (ii), Special Tables for Sechedule Tribes, pp. 40-97 and 186.

12. Census of India, 1971, *Social and Cultural Tables* (Table VII and VIII) Part II-C (1), Series -18, Rajasthan, pp. 604-693.

13. Census of India, 1981, series-18, Part IX Special Tables for S.T., pp. 8-15.

14. Census of India, 1981, Series-18, Part-IX, Special Tables for S.T., pp. 8-195.

15. Bendict, R: The Study of Cultural Continuities in the Infleunce of Home and Community on Children under Thirteen Years of Age (Paris, UNESCO, p. 8.)

16. Mead, M: *Research on Primitive Children* in L. Carmichael: Manual of Child Psychology, New York, 1946, pp. 667-706.

18. Johnson. H.M.: Sociology, 1963, p. 112.

19. Raj S. Mobinuddin, *The Process of Socialization. A Multy Ethnic Study*, Chetana Publications, New Delhi, p. 6.

20. Stuart and Prugh: *The Healthy Child, his Physical, Psychological, and Social Development*, Harvard University Press, Sixth Printing, 1973, p. 66.

21. *Ibid.*, p. 41.

22. *Ibid.*, p. 82.

23. Marian E. Breckentridge & Vincent E. Lee, *Child Development: Physical and Psychological Growh through Adolescence* (Fifth Edition) W.B. Saunders Company. Philadelphia and London p. 41-42.

24. *Ibid.*, p. 42.

25. *Ibid.*, p. 43.

26. Richards, Martin: *Infancy-world of the Newborn, Multimedia* Publications Inc. Willemstend (Curacao) 1980, p.10.

27. Bahadur, K.P. *Caste & Culture of India Vol. IV*. Karnataka. Kerala & Tamil Nadu, Ess Ess Publication, New Delhi, 1978, p. 73-79.

28. *Ibid*.

29. *Ibid*.

30. *Ibid*.

31. *Ibid.*
32. *Ibid.*
33. Choudhary, N.C.; *Munda Social Structure*, Firmak L.M. Private Limited, Calcutta, 1977, pp. 70-74.
34. Vidyarthi and Rai, *The Tribal Culture of India*, p. 293 & 295 Chaudhuri, Buddhadab (Ed.),.
35. *Tribal Health—Socio Cultural Dimensions*, (1988), Inter India Pub., New Delhi, pp. 147.
36. Future 24-25, Spring-Summer 1988, A UNICEF Quarterly, p. 52.
37. Furure, 1982. First Quarter, p. 47.
38. 2 Future-21, 1987, p. 22-23.
39. *Ibid.*, p. 26.
40. Rechard W.B. Ellis (Ed.): *Child Health and Development*, Fourth Edition, J & A Churchill Ltd., London, 1966, p. 143-145.
41. Stuart and Prugh: *The Healthy Child: His Physical, Psychological and Social Development*, Harward University Press (Sixth Printing,) 1973, p. 143-145.
42. *Manual for Child Nutrition in Rural India*, Ed. by. Cecile D. Sweemer., Nandita Sen Gupta, Sheila B. Takulia; Published by Voluntany Health Association of India, New Delhi, 1978, pp. 131-132.
43. *Ibid.*, p. 133.
44. 2 Future 21, 1987, p. 23.
45. Richard W.B. Ells (Ed.) *Child Health and Development*, Fourth Edition, J & A Churchill Ltd. London, 1966, p. 104.
46.. *Ibid.*, p. 124.
47. Stuart and Prugh: *The Healthy Child: His Physical, Psychological and Social Development*, Harward University Press (Sixth Printing) 1973, p. 157.
48. Poul H. Mussen, John J. Conger and Jerome Kagan: *Child Development and Personality*. (Fourth Edition, Harper and Row Publishers, New York, 1974, p. 108.
49. *Manual for Child Nutrition in Rural India* Published by Voluntary Health Association of India, New Delhi, 1978, p. 138.
50. Richard W.B. Ellis (ED.) *Child Health and Development*, Fourth Edition, J & A Churchill, London, 1966, p. 124-126.

51. *Ibid.*, p. 126.

52. Marian E. Brecken-lidge & Vincent E. Lee, *Child Development: Phychological Growth* through Addesence (Fifth Edition) W.B. Saunders Company, Philadelphia and London, pp. 125-126.

53. *Ibid.*, p.126.

54. *Ibid.*, pp. 124-125.

55. 2 Future - 21, 1987, p. 24.

56. *Ibid.*, p. 31.

57. *Ibid.*, p. 31.

58. Stuart and Prugh: *The Healthy Child : His Physical, Psychological and Social Development*, Harward University Press (Sixth Printing) 1973, p. 23.

2 Demographic Profile

With Special Reference to Rajasthan

The tribal aborigines have always been an attraction for adventurous people. Since 1951 social change started percolating in the life of these tribals because of the various government sponsored Community Development Programmes. Though all the tribals could not change, but they moved towards rapid acculturation.

The tribals are an intrinsic part of our national life and with their rich cultural heritage they have been contributing a lot to the complex amalgam. The tribals settled down in India in prehistoric times, inhabiting mostly the sparsely populated part of in the mountain belt of central India between, Narmada & Godavari rivers, and in the southern pats of the Western Ghats extending from Wynad to Kanyakumari.

The tribals are primitive and live in isolation *i.e.* in dense forests which are generally cut off from civilised area. Hence, Tribals have limited contact with other societies. The practice of isolation helps them to preserve their social customs, traditions and beliefs to a large extent.

The territorial distribution of many tribes overlaps the political boundaries of the state and territory. For a better understanding of the demographic situation of the tribals, the states and territories have been classified into seven regions as mentioned below:

1. *North-eastern Region:* This region comprises the states of Arunachal Pradesh, Assam, Manipur, Meghalaya, Mizoram, Nagaland and Tripura.

2. *Eastern Region:* This region includes the states of Bihar, Orissa, Sikkim and West Bengal.
3. *Northern Region:* This region belongs to the states of Himachal Pradesh and Uttar Pradesh.
4. *Central Region :* This region consists of only one states *i.e.* Madhaya Pradesh.
5. *Western Region:* This region is the part of the states of Rajasthan, Maharashtra, Gujarat, Dadar and Nagar Haveli, Goa, Daman and Diu.
6. *Southern region:* This region comprises of the states of Andhra Pradesh, Karnataka, Tamil Nadu and Kerala.
7. *Island Region:* This region constitutes Andaman and Nicobar Island, and Lakshadweep.

According to 1951 census, the Scheduled Tribes' population in India was 1,91,47,054 which constituted 5.3 per cent of the total population of the country. After the Scheduled Tribes' Lists modification order, 1956 tribal population rose to 2,25,11,845 or 6.23 per cent. This increase of 34 lakhs in the population of tribals was due to the inclusion of certain groups. According to 1961 census, the tribal populaton was 3,04,30,184 *i.e.,* 6.86 per cent of the total population. As per 1971 census the Scheduled Tribe population was 3.80 millions while the total populaton was 54.8 millions. This formed 6.94 per cent of the total population. The above census figures indicate the regular increase in tribal population. The Scheduled Tribe list was again amended in 1976 vide order No. 108 of 18th Sept. 1976.

According to 1981 census 5,16,28,638 persons were enumerated in the country excluding Assam where the census was not held due to unavoidable conditions. The Scheduled Tribes constitute 2,60,38,535 males and 2,55,90,103 females. The Scheduled tribe population constitute only, 7.76 per cent of the total population of the country. The state-wise break-up of the tribal population. According to 1981, 1991 and 2001 census is given in Table 2.1 and 2.2, which reveals that the tribals were enumerated throughout the country, except in the state of Haryana, Jammu & Kashmir, Punjab, Chandigarh, Delhi and Pondicherry where the tribals are not Scheduled, the North eastern region is highly concentrated with tribal. According to 2001 census the tribal population of the country was 8.2 per cent of the total population—which shows 0.44 per cent increase in tribal population during last three decades.

Rajasthan

Rajasthan is one of the major state in India where concentration of tribal population is high. The dominating tribals of the state are Mina, Bhil, Garasia, Sahariya and Damor. The tribals are found throughout the state *i.e.* in all the districts. But the southern part of the state characterised by the Aravali range has been the primary home of tribals.

According to the Scheduled Tribes' Amendment order 1976, the following 12 groups of tribes were listed as under—

(1) Bhil, Bhil Garasia, Dholi Bhil, Dungri Bhil, Dungari Garasia, Mewashi Bhil, Rawal Bhil, Tadvi Bhil, Bhagalia, Bhilala, Pawara, Vasava, Vasave.

(2) Bhil-Mina

(3) Damor, Damaria

(4) Dhanka, Tadvi, Tetaria, Valvi

(5) Garasia (excluding Rajput Garasia)

(6) Kathodi, Katkari, Dhor Kathodi, Dhor Kathari, Son Kathodi, Son Katkari.

(7) Kokna, Kokni, Kukna

(8) Koli Dhor, Tokre Koli, Kolgha, Kolgha

(9) Mina

(10) Naikda, Nayaka, Cholivala Nayaka, Kapadia Nayaka, Mota Nayaka, Nana Nayaka

(11) Patelia

(12) Seharia, Sehria, Sahariya.

The total population of the state according to 2001 census was 56,507,188 (29,420,011, Male and 27,087,177 Female). The total tribal population according to 2001 census was 7,097,706 (3,650,982 male and 3,446,724 female) which constitutes 12.56 per cent of the state's total population. According to 2001 census the total population was 565,507,188 persons (29,420,011 males and 27,087,177 female), while the tribal population was 7,097,706 persons (3,650,982 male and 3,446,724 female) which constitute 12.56 per cent of the state population. The detail is discussed in Table 2.3 (p. 51) and 2.4 (p. 52). The tribe-wise population from 1961 to 1991 is detailed is the given Table 2.5 (p. 53) and 2.6 (p. 56).

The Table 2.5 (p. 53) reveals that 7,74,036 tribals has been increased according to 1971 census this increase was about 32.92 per cent to the 1961 S.T. population and 10,57,618 were added to the previous population of S.T. at the time of 1981 census *i.e.* the increase was 33.84 per cent to the 1971 S.T. population. The increase was just double of the 1961 S.T. population. According to 1971 census the S.T. population was 12.13 per cent while in 1981 the S.T. population was 12.21 per cent. Hence the increase was very low *i.e.* 0.08 per cent only. Thus we can say that the growth rate of the general population was very high in comparison to the S.T. population.

This table also indicates that Minas constitute the highest percentage *i.e.* 2.84 per cent, Seharia stands fourth *i.e.* 0.98 per cent and Damor stands fifth *i.e.* 0.75 per cent while the list Kokna, Kokni occupy the lowest position in the rank. They have a negligible percentage *i.e.* 0.004 per cent only. Similar trend was observed in 1991 census.

The category-wise and district-wise distribution of tribals according to 1981 census is given in Table-2.7 (p. 55).

The table reveals that Bhil, Mina Nakia and Nayak are found throughout the state. The district of Banswara stands, firstand it covers 72.63 per cent, Dungarpur stands seond *i.e.* 64.44 per cent Udaipur stands third *i.e.* 34.33 per cent Sirohi stands fourth *i.e.* 23.11 per cent Sawai-Madhopur stands fifth *i.e.* 22.67 per cent of their total population. The lowest concentrated area is tha of Bikaner and Nagaur having only 0.18 per cent of their total population. Hence, we can say that the tribals are spread more or less everywhere in the state.

Population by Sex

According to 1981 census, the state of Rajasthan has 41,83,124 persons of tribal population. Out of this, 21,50,767 were males and 20,32,357 were females. In the state out of 3,42,61,862 persons, 1,78,54,154 were males and 1,64,07,708 females. Of the total population, the males constitutes 12.05 per cent while females constitutes 12.39 per cent to the total state male and female population respectively. It shows that in triballs the female population is higher than the male population in comparison to the total population.

In Rajasthan according to 1981 census, females per 1000 males among the total ST. population was 945 while in Rural area, it was 952 and 785 in urban area respectively.

Marital Status

In tribals, except Minas, the main base of marriage is Brideprice *i.e.* "dapa" In Minas' marriage is generally arranged by the parents at early age the dowery system exists among them. In other tribes polygamy also exists but it is not so in the Minas.

In tribals widow marriage and Nata system is very common. Divorce is also prevalent in the society and it cause ulitmately Nata. The Nata is also based on bride price which is called "Jagada".

The tribe wise marital status of the tribals datailed in Table 2.8 (page 59).

Table 2.1: State-wise Distribution of Tribals in India, 1981

Sl. No.	State Union Territories	Total population	Scheduled Tribes population			% of ST Population to total population
			Male	Female	Persons	
1	2	3	4	5	6	7
	India	665,287,849	26,038,535	25,590,103	51,628,638	7.76
1.	Andhra Pradesh	53,549,673	1,618,689	1,557,312	3,176,001	5.93
2.	Bihar	69,914,734	2,915,492	2,895,375	5,810,867	8.31
3.	Gujarat	34,085,799	2,453,566	2,395,020	4,848,586	14.22
4.	Haryana	12,922,618	—	—	—	—
5.	Himachal Pradesh	4,280,818	99,727	97,536	197,263	4.61
6.	Jammu & Kashmir	5,987,389	—	—	—	—
7.	Karnataka	37,135,714	926,235	895,968	1,825,203	4.91
8.	Kerala	25,453,680	131,243	130,232	261,475	1.03
9.	Madhya Pradesh	52,178,844	6,003,304	5,983,727	11,987,031	22.97
10.	Maharashtra	62,784,171	2,923,955	2,848,083	5,772,038	9.19
11.	Manipur	1,420,953	196,455	191,522	387,977	27.30
12.	Meghalaya	1,355,819	537,635	538,710	1,076,345	80.58
13.	Nagaland	774,930	332,943	317,942	650,885	83.99
14.	Orissa	26,370,271	2,939,863	2,975,204	5,915,067	22.43
15.	Rajasthan	34,261,862	2,150,767	2,032,357	4,183,124	12.21
16.	Sikkim	316,385	38,211	35,412	73,623	23.27
17.	Tamil Nadu	48.408,077	264,288	255,938	520,226	1.07
18.	Tripura	2,053,058	297,612	286,308	583,920	28.44
19.	Uttar Pradesh	110,862,013	121,506	111,199	232,705	00.21
20.	Punjab	16,788,985	—	—	—	—
21.	West Bengal	154,580,647	1,559,288	1,511,368	3,070,672	5.63
	Union-territories					
1.	Andaman & Nicobar Isaland	188,741	11,586	10,775	22,361	11.85
2.	Arunachal Pradesh	631,839	220,046	221,121	441,167	69.82

1	2	3	4	5	6	7
3.	Dadar and Nagar Haveli	103,676	40,486	41,228	81,714	18.82
4.	Chandigarh	451,610	—	—	—	—
5.	Delhi	6,220,406	—	—	—	—
6.	Goa, Daman and Diu	1,086,730	5,512	5,209	10,711	0.99
7.	Lakshadweep	40,249	18,865	18,895	37,760	93.82
8.	Mizoram	493,757	231,261	230,646	461,907	93.55
9.	Pondicherry	604,471	—	—	—	—

Source: 1. Census of India 1981, Series-1, Part-II-B (iii) Primary Census Abstract (Scheduled Tribes), pp. XIXXXI and 4-15.

2. Census of India 1981, Series-1, Part-II-B (i) Primary Census Abstract (General population) pp. XXXXXXIII and 4-23.

Table 2.2: State-wise Distribution of Tribals in India (Census 1991 & 2001)

Sl. No.	India/ State	Total population 1991	Total population 2001	ST population 1991	ST population 2001	%age of STs in the State to total ST population 2001 census	%age of STs in the State to total ST population 2001 census
1	2	3	4	5	6	7	8
0	India	838,583,988	1,028,610,328	67,758,380	84,326,240	8.2	—
1.	Andhra Pradesh	66,508,008	76,210,007	4,199,481	5,024,104	6.6	5.96
2.	Arunachal Pradesh	864,558	1,097,968	550,351	705,158	64.2	0.84
3.	Assam	22,414,322	26,655,528	2,874,441	3.308,570	12.4	3.92
4.	Bihar	86,374,465	82,998,509	6,616,914	758,351	0.9	0.90
5.	Chhattisgarh		20,833,803		6,616,596	31.8	7.85
6.	Goa	1,169,793	1,347,668	376	566		0.07

1	2	3	4	5	6	7	8
7.	Gujrat	41,309,582	50,671,017	6,161,775	7,481,160	14.8	8.87
8.	Haryana	16.463.648	21.144.564				
9.	Himachal Pradesh	5.170.877	6.077.900	218.349	244.587	4.0	0.29
10.	Jharkhand		26,945,829		7,087,068	26.3	8.40
11.	Karnataka	44.977.201	52.850.562	1.915.691	3.463.986	6.6	4.11
12.	Kerala	29.098.518	31.841.374	320.967	364.189	1.1	0.43
13.	Madhya Pradesh	66.181,170	60.348,023	15,399,034	12.233.474	20.3	14.51
14.	Maharashtra	78.937.187	96.878.627	7.318.281	8.577.276	8.9	10.17
15.	Manipur	1.837.149	2166.788	632.173	741.141	34.2	0.88
16.	Meghalaya	1.774.778	2.318.822	1.517.927	1.992.862	85.9	2.36
17.	Mizoram	689,756	888,573	653,565	839,310	94,5	1.00
18.	Nagaland	1,209,546	1,990,036	1.060.822	1.774.026	89.1	2.10
19.	Orissa	31.659.736	36.804.660	7.032.214	8.145.081	22.1	9.66
20.	Punjab	20.281.969	24.358.999	0			
21.	Rahasthan	44.005.990	56.507.188	5.474.881	7.097.706	12.6	8.42
22.	Sikkim	406.457	540.851	90.901	111.405	20.6	0.13
23.	TamilNadu	55.858.946	62.405.679	574.194	651.321	1.0	0.77
24.	Tripura	2.757.205	3.199.203	853.345	993.426	31.1	1.18
25.	Uttranchal		8.489.349		256.129	3.0	0.30
26.	Uttar Pradesh	139.112.287	166.197.921	287.901	107.963	0.1	0.13
27.	West Bengal	68.077.965	80.176.197	3.808.760	4.406.794	5.5	5.23
28.	Andman & Nicobar Island	280.661	356.152	26.770	29.469	8.3	0.03
29.	Chandigarh	642.015	900.635	0			
30.	Dadra & Nagar Haveli	138.477	220.490	109.380	137.255	62.2	0.16
31.	Daman & Diu	101.586	158.204	11.724	13.997	8.8	
32.	Delhi	9.420.644	13.850.507	0	NST		
33.	Lakshadweep	51.707	60.650	48.163	57.321	94.5	0.07
34.	Pondicherry	807.785	974.345	0			
35.	Jammu and Kashmir		10.143.700		1.105.979		
	Total	838,583,988	1,028,610,328	67,758,380	84,326,240		

State like Chhattisgarh, Jharkhand and Uttaranchal were created in the year 2000 after reorganisation of Madhya Pradesh, Bihar and Uttar Pradesh.

Table 2.3: Rajasthan at a Glance (Census-2001)
District-wise Total & S.T. Population, 2001

Sl.No.	District	Total Population			Scheduled Tribes Populaton			% of S.T. to Total Population
		Person	Male	Female	Person	Male	Female	
1	2	3	4	5	6	7	8	9
1.	Ajmer	2181670	1129920	1051750	52634	27346	25288	2.41
2.	Alwar	2992592	1586752	1405840	239905	127707	1121198	8.02
3.	Banswara	1501589	760686	740903	1085272	547277	537995	72.27
4.	Baran	1021653	535137	486516	216869	113058	103811	21.23
5.	Barmer	1964835	1038247	926588	118688	62938	5575	6.04
6.	Bharatpur	2101142	1133425	967717	47077	25195	21882	2.24
7.	Bhilwara	2013789	1026650	987139	180556	93089	87467	8.97
8.	Bikaner	1674271	886075	788196	5945	3272	2673	0.36
9.	Bundi	962620	504818	457802	194851	102678	92173	20.24
10.	Chittaurgarh	1803524	918063	885461	388311	197416	190895	21.53
11.	Churu	1923878	987781	936097	10063	5339	4724	0.52
12.	Dausa	1317063	693438	623625	353187	186464	166723	26.82
13.	Dhaulpur	983258	538103	445155	47612	25954	21658	4.84
14.	Dungarpur	1107643	547791	559852	721487	355748	365739	65.14
15.	Ganganagar	1789423	955378	834045	14744	7948	6796	0.82
16.	Hanumangarh	1518005	801486	716519	10029	5367	4662	0.66
17.	Jaipur	5251071	2768203	2482868	412864	217546	195318	7.86
18.	Jaisalmer	508247	279101	229146	27834	14890	12944	5.48
19.	Jalor	1448940	737880	711060	126799	66610	60189	8.75
20.	Jhalawar	1180323	612804	567519	141861	74014	67847	12.02
21.	Jhunjhunun	1913689	983526	930163	36794	19054	17740	1.92
22.	Jodhpur	2886505	1513890	1372615	79540	41450	38090	2.76
23.	Karauli	1209665	651998	557667	270630	145962	124668	22.37
24.	Kota	1568525	827128	741397	151969	80616	71353	9.69
25.	Nagaur	2775058	1424967	1350091	6497	3503	2994	0.23

1	2	3	4	5	6	7	8	9
26.	Pail	1820251	918856	901395	105814	54928	50886	5.81
27.	Rajsamand	987024	493459	493565	129198	65657	63541	13.09
28.	Sawai Madhopur	1117057	591307	525750	241078	128446	112632	21.58
29.	Sikar	2287788	1172753	1115035	62512	32493	30019	2.73
30.	Sirohi	851107	437949	413158	210763	107905	102858	24.76
31.	Tonk	1211671	626436	585235	145891	76159	69732	12.04
32.	Udaipur	2633312	1336004	1297308	1260432	634653	625479	47.86
	Total	56507188	29420011	27087177	7097706	3650982	3446724	12.56

Table 2.4:Tribal Sub Plan Area of Rajasthan (Census 2001)

Total & S.T. Population of T.S.P. Area According to Total, Rural, Urban & Sex wise

Sl. No.	District of Scheduled Area	Total Rural Urban	Total Population			S.T. Population			% of S.T. to Total population	Sex Ratio	
			Persons	Males	Females	Persons	Males	Females		S.T.	Total
1.	Udaipur	T	1433565	719289	714276	1013728	508272	505456	70.71	994	993
		R	1381320	692219	689101	1008183	505350	502833	72.99	995	995
		U	52245	27070	25175	5545	2922	2623	10.61	898	930
2.	Banswara	T	1501589	760686	740903	1085272	547277	537995	72.27	933	974
		R	1394226	705110	689116	1073930	541412	532518	77.03	984	977
		U	107363	55576	51787	11342	5865	5477	10.56	934	932
3.	Dungarpur	T	1107643	547791	559852	721487	355748	365736	65.14	1028	1022
		R	1026787	505664	521123	703877	346558	357319	68.55	1031	1031
		U	80856	42127	38729	17610	9190	8420	21.78	916	919
4.	Chittaurgarh	T	356488	182091	174397	196213	99754	96459	55.04	967	958
		R	321066	163614	157452	193772	98399	95373	60.35	969	962
		U	35422	18477	16945	2441	1355	1086	6.89	801	917
5.	Sirohi	T	114818	59326	55492	76526	38864	37662	66.65	969	935
		R	114818	59326	55492	76526	38864	37662	66.65	969	935
		U	-	-	-	-	-	-	-	-	-
	Total	T	**4514103**	**2269183**	**2244920**	**3093226**	**1549915**	**1543311**	**68.52**	**996**	**989**
		R	4238217	2125933	2112284	3056288	1530583	1525705	72.11	994	994
		U	**275886**	**143250**	**132636**	**36938**	**19332**	**17606**	**13.39**	**911**	**926**
6.	Rajasthan	T	56507188	29420011	27087177	7097706	3650982	3446724	12.56	944	921
		R	43292813	22426640	20866173	6717830	3445719	3272111	15.52	950	930
		U	13214375	6993371	6221004	379876	205263	174613	2.87	851	890

Table 2.5:Tribe-wise Population (1961 – 1981)

Sl. No.	Tribe	1961[1]	1971[2]	1981[3]			% of total S.T. population
				Male	Female	Persons (total)	
	Rajasthan	2,351,470	3,125,506	2,150,767	2,032,357	4,183,124	100
1.	Bhil, Bhil Garasia, Dholi Bhil, Dungri Bhil Dungri Garasia, Mewasi Bhil, Rawal Bhil, Tadvi Bhil, Bhagalia, Bhilala, Pawra, Vasava, Vasava	906,705	1,437,937	929,087	911,879	1,840,966	44.01
2.	Bhil–Mina	2063	17,076	13,766	13,371	27,137	0.65
3.	Damor, Damaria	14,534	14,795	15,937	15,440	31,377	0.75
4.	Dhanka, Tadvi, Tetaria, Valvi	—	157	7,378	6,733	14,11	0.34
5.	Garasia (exculding Rajput Garasia	62,509	52,268	60,225	58,332	118,757	2.84
6.	Kathodi, Katkari, Dhor Kathodi, Dhor Katkari, Son Kathodi, Son Katkari	—	1	1,236	1,317	2,553	0.06
7.	Kokna, Kohni, Kukna	—	2	91	74	165	Neg. (0.004)
8.	Koli Dhor, Tokre Koli Kolcha, Kolgha	—	166	1,075	1,006	2,081	0.05
9.	Mina	1,155,620	1,532,331	1,091,451	995,241	2,086,692	49.88
10.	Naikda, Nayaka, Cholivala Nayaka, Kapadia Nayaka, Mota Nayaka, Nana Nayaka	—	32	4,800	4,347	9,174	0.22
11.	Patelia	—	1	931	772	1,703	0.04
12.	Seharia, Sehria, Sahariya	23,299	26,939	20,821	20,124	40,945	0.98
13.	Unspecified	186,740	43,801	3,969	3,494	7,463	0.18

Source:
1. Census of India, 1961 Vol.–I India, Part V-A (ii) Special Tables for Scheduled Tribes pp 40–97 & 186.
2. Census of India, 1971, Social and Cultural Tables (Table VII & VIII) Part II–C (i), Series–18, Rajasthan, pp. 604–693.
3. Census of India, 1981, Series–18, Part–IX, Special Tables for S.T. pp 8–15.

Table 2.6:Table-wise Population (1991)

(Number)

Sl.No.	State/District		Production		
	Rajasthan		Total	Males	Females
1	2		3	4	4
	All Scheduled Tribes	Total	54,74,881	28,37,014	26,37,867
		Rural	52,20,549	26,96,437	25,24,112
		Urban	2,54,332	1,40,577	1,13,755
1.	Bhil, Bhil Garasia, Dholi Bhil, Dungri Bhil, Dungri Garasia.....	Total	23,05,982	11,77,865	11,28,117
		Rural	22,28,487	11,36,860	10,91,627
		Urban	77,495	41,005	36,490
2.	Bhil Mina	Total	32,592	16,678	15,914
		Rural	28,733	14,562	14,171
		Urban	3,859	2,116	1,743
3.	Damor, Damaria	Total	43,612	21,801	21,811
		Rural	42,525	21,189	21,336
		Urban	1,087	612	475
4.	Dhanka, Tadvi, Tetaria, Valvi	Total	33,844	17,990	15,854
		Rural	14,493	7,742	6,751
		Urban	19,351	10,248	9,103
5.	Garasia (excluding Rajput Garasia)	Total	1,48,197	75,899	72,298
		Rural	1,47,303	75,332	71,971
		Urban	894	567	327
6.	Kathodi, Katkari, Dhor Kathodi, Dhor Katkari, ...	Total	2,984	1,498	1,486
		Rural	2,893	1,444	1,449
		Urban	91	54	37
7.	Kokna, Kokni, Kukna	Total	710	378	332
		Rural	609	322	287
		Urban	101	56	45

1	2		3	4	4
8.	Koli Dhor, Tokre Koli, Koleha, Kolgha	Total	2,973	1,576	1,397
		Rural	2,549	1,339	1,210
		Urban	424	237	187
9.	Mina	Total	27,99,167	14,69,158	13,30,000
		Rural	26,58,344	13,89,085	12,69,250
		Urban	1,40,823	80,073	60,750
10.	Naikda, Nayaka, Cholivala Nayaka, Kapadia Nayaka	Total	11,627	6,272	5,355
		Rural	7,859	4,177	3,682
		Urban	3,768	2,095	1,673
11.	Patelia	Total	2,554	1,074	1,480
		Rural	1,977	763	1,214
		Urban	577	311	266
12.	Seharia, Saharia, Sahariya	Total	59,810	30,555	29,255
		Rural	58,749	30,011	28,738
		Urban	1,061	544	517
13.	Unclassified	Total	30,829	16,270	14,559
		Rural	26,028	13,611	12,417
		Urban	4,801	2,659	2,142

Source: Census of India, 1991.

Table 2.7: Categories-wise and District-wise Distribution of Scheduled Tribes

(Number)

S.No.	State/ District	All Scheduled Tribes	Bhil, ...	Bhil, Mina	Damor, Damia	Dhanka, Tadvi, ...	Garasia	Kathodi Katkari, ...
1	2	3	4	5	6	7	8	9
	Rajasthan	4183124	1840966	27137	31377	14111	118757	2553
1.	Ganganagar	5095	525	45	6	898	74	23

1	2	3	4	5	6	7	8	9
2.	Bikaner	1496	423	—	—	2	23	—
3.	Churu	5619	82	5	—	285	5	8
4.	Jhunjhunu	23077	94	27	—	440	—	3
5.	Alwar	143858	369	1	—	1267	2	2
6.	Bharatpur	56716	514	1	—	—	—	—
7.	Sawai Madhopur	348130	1132	76	28	52	22	4
8.	Jaipur	380199	1668	40	22	7593	22	7
9.	Sikar	36552	11	—	—	708	14	—
10.	Ajmer	23183	17608	15	1	2159	8	12
11.	Tonk	92477	7612	2	5	3	1	2
12.	Jaisalmer	10680	10532	48	3	—	8	—
13.	Jodhpur	28288	37559	179	2	74	34	5
14.	Nagaur	2984	221	—	—	43	1	—
15.	Pali	69694	15069	66	2	10	20223	1
16.	Barmer	57038	56344	19	1	—	1	—
17.	Jalor	72361	57111	14	1	—	70	—
18.	Sirohi	125245	51420	16	4	41	58484	1
19.	Bhilwara	121664	69113	12	5	25	103	5
20.	Udaipur	809156	392709	2147	1153	18	38325	1919
21.	Chittaurgrah	223864	80687	191	530	185	277	10
22.	Dungarpur	440026	131871	3307	22240	4	192	9
23.	Banswara	643866	582723	20875	7316	51	838	—
24.	Bundi	118030	23760	5	2	—	—	—
25.	Kota	231316	49950	36	55	247	30	379
26.	Jhalawar	91601	51863	7	1	4	—	162

Table 2.7: Categories-wise and District-wise Distribution of Scheduled Tribes-*Contd.*

(Number)

Sl.No.	State/ District	Katana, Kokni, ...	Koli, Dhor, ...	Mina	Naika, Nayaka, ...	Patelia	Seharia, Sehria, Sahariya	Percentage S.T. to total population
1	2	10	11	12	13	14	15	16
	Rajasthan	165	2081	2086692	9174	1703	40945	12.21
1.	Ganganagar	18	1	2950	406	3	20	0.25
2.	Bikaner	—	—	456	556	—	—	0.18
3.	Churu	1	—	4960	200	—	4	0.48
4.	Jhunjhunu	1	—	22265	213	—	—	1.90
5.	Alwar	4	159	141939	100	—	—	8.12
6.	Bharatpur	4	128	55819	13	—	168	3.01
7.	Sawai Madhopur	7	505	346097	64	—	12	22.67
8.	Jaipur	12	233	368024	2283	1	7	11.12
9.	Sikar	9	1	35560	263	—	—	2.65
10.	Ajmer	11	—	11860	433	35	—	2.23
11.	Tonk	—	—	11860	433	35	—	2.23
12.	Jaisalmer	1	—	36	31	—	—	4.39
13.	Jodhpur	4	31	672	1338	—	—	2.40
14.	Nagaur	2	—	2341	324	—	—	0.18
15.	Pali	6	57	33865	197	8	—	5.47
16.	Barmer	2	—	451	17	3	—	5.10
17.	Jalor	12	231	14834	1	21	11	8.01
18.	Sirohi	1	439	14550	21	102	1	23.11
19.	Bhilwara	15	21	51837	441	26	10	9.28
20.	Udaipur	12	—	370519	177	31	178	34.33
21.	Chittaurgrah	12	55	140578	496	137	474	18.16

1	2	10	11	12	13	14	15	16
22.	Dungarpur	7	5	81971	29	9	—	64.44
23.	Banswara	8	—	29544	46	348	5	72.63
24.	Bundi	2	31	93826	265	114	1	20.11
25.	Kota	6	168	138687	1026	497	39808	14.83
26.	Jhalawar	7	13	38297	178	367	247	11.67

Source: Census of India, 1981, Series-18, Part-IX, Special Tables for S.T., pp. 8—195.

Table 2.8: Tribe-wise Marital Status of the Tribals

(Number)

Sl.No.	Tribe	Total		Never Married		Married		Widowed		Divorced or separated	
		Male	Female	Male	Female	Male	Female	Male	Female	Male	Female
	Rajasthan	2150767	2032357	1134606	929009	953846	982161	57040	117311	4826	2782
1.	Bhil, Bhil-Garasia	929087	911879	497721	435636	408759	425059	19590	46079	2810	1592
2.	Bhil–Mina	13765	13371	7637	6726	5864	5946	228	675	33	15
3.	Damor, Damaria	15937	15440	8382	7327	7097	7362	373	683 8	0	54
4.	Dhanka, Tadvi, Tetaria, Valvi	7377	6733	3927	2919	3289	3329	155	478	7	5
5.	Garasia	60225	58532	33774	30354	24866	25870	1356	2126	221	157
6.	Kathodi, Katkari,.........	1236	1317	686	707	536	565	14	45	—	—
7.	Kokna, Kokni, Kukna	92	74	38	25	49	44	4	4	—	—
8.	Koli Dhor, Tokre Koli, Kolcha, ...	1074	1006	590	465	549	479	25	61	—	1
9.	Mina	1091451	995241	566389	432335	488538	499184	34696	62270	1610	933
10.	Naikda, Nayaka,....	4800	4374	2512	1874	2183	2183	95	311	8	3
11.	Patelia	931	772	451	379	459	365	15	27	3	—
12.	Seharia, Sehria, Sahariya	20821	20124	10339	8640	10035	10110	395	1349	50	17

3 Child Development Processes

In the context of the development and integration of tribals, it must be observed that the rearing, upbringing and socialization of the infants assume crucial importance. It is useful to see that the development of tribals also takes into consideration the development of the infants. In fact, the infants are the coming generation who will have to carry forward the legacy of development and integration. Physiologists argue that, the formative period for any personality lies some where between 5 to 16 years. If the tribal infants are socialized right from the beginning within the secular democratic and socialistic frame work, the coming tribal society would be much nearer to the mainstream. Yet another problem which the tribals face today is the crisis of cultural identity whereby they strive to retain some of their premordial ethic traits.

The present enquiry is concerned with the study of child rearing or development and socializing practices of the dominating tribal group Bhil of the Tribal sub-plan area, the only one of the state of Rajasthan. The Bhils are basically dwellers of hills and forests. Their century long isolation has provided to them a specific identity to child rearing and socializing practices. Every society assures the continuity of its culture through child rearing habits. It is in this context that the socializing practices of tribals are very important. Actually it is the socialization which provides continuity and survival to the community, when we differentiate the tribal society from the non-tribal it is the specific ethnicity of the tribals, which gives differentiation. As a matter of fact the Bhil society has certain perimordial ethic traits which are handed down to the coming generation by the process of rearing and socialization. If we accept this hypothesis, it would mean that the development values and traits can also be given to the tribal personality through processes of socialization. The main premise of our enquiry is to find out the nexus between the values norms and structures of the traditional society and the new values of structures of the secular and democratic society in terms of the socialization and rearing of tribal infants.

A knowledge of growth would be meaningless without some understanding of the substrances which go to make up the individual and the force, within and without, which set the direction and pace of growth or development *i.e.* rearing practices. Through knowing the factors which effect growth, then parents can open the way to optimal development for children by providing satisfactory, environment and guidance. Environment includes habits of living such as keeping, eating, activity and adjustment with the circumstance and the surroundings *i.e.* with the other family members. The factors need be more carefully controlled for infants with a familial tendency for a healthy background.

All children have certain needs for growth *i.e.* development. All children do not get these needs in the same manner, but some of them may get the required needs fully of partially children will differ in sleep and activity requirements and in sensitivity to emotional stimuli.

The child development practices are different in the tribals in comparison to non-tribals. In the non-tribals, are well to do and connected with the more socialized families or have knowledge of the child rearing practices, while the tribals are isolated, and have their traditional traits. There is no change in their traditional followings. They do not have medical facilities nearby their residence or their dwellings.

In this chapter we have discuss the child development practices adopted in Bhil society from inception to infancy *i.e.* upto the age of four years without making any sex difference. The rearing practices in Bhil society is quite different to non-tribals, but they are not abnormal.

In Bhil society every couple wishes for child either male or female, without any discrimination. The female child is treated equally good, because she helps in the domestic work as well as support the family economically. The second reason is that 'Bride Price' locally known as "Papa" is charged from the "groom" side, in case of divorce, they get all the expenses of the marriage to the boy side, after divorce the girl can remarry and the father gets "bride price" again. In this society "Nata" is also common, in this system a married women can go with any other person or her lover, with paying her cost knows as "Jagda". In this manner the girl is treated beneficial for their parents and after marriage for their husband's.

The stage of childlessness is despised by them. It is believed that childless persons, more particularly those who are without sons, cannot prosper. It is, however, believed that mere physical union of male and female *i.e.* a couple is not sufficient for conception, for the blessing of the deities. They also believe that some malevolent deities and spirit can also frustrate a couples efforts to be blessed by the offsprings. In case of childlessness. They generally approached to *Bheru* and *Bhopa* to findout the reasons and also remedy for infertility, abortions and mortality of infants.

The first conception is treated very good and they fell very pleasure, while they treat others are also good. Regarding conceptions their view that more children will be helpful for more earnings.

There are no rites to be observed between the period from conception to the maturity of the pregnancy *i.e.* upto the birth of child or delivery takes places. The conception is assumed by stopping the menstruation and starting of vomiting and is confirmed by the *dais* or the old ladies of the families by examining the womb of the expectant mother.

In Bhil society the females contribute in economy equally, so they generally work for a long time till they can do easily. In some cases the expectant mother goes for work upto few hours before delivery. The expectant mother also do all domestic work before few hours of the delivery, while in other societies expectant mother stops the hard work during the fifth month of the pregnancy, they are forced to do hard work, because of poor economic condition.

Food during Pregnancy

During pregnancy the expectant mother takes regular diet as she takes in normal days. But the frequency increased by one more *i.e.* she takes meals thrice daily. During pregnancy no special food is given to the expectant mother.

Precautions during Pregnancy

During pregnancy the expectant mother avoids heavy weight lifting in the last months of the pregnancy, it is believed that by lifting heavy weighs miscarriage may be.

During the last months of pregnancy the expectant mother avoids to eat fatty things *e.g.* Banana, Black gram pulse (Uradki–Dal), curd, etc.

Delivery

In Bhil society generally the first delivery takes place at the parents house of the expectant mother, rest deliveries takes place at their own house.

The delivery is generally performed by the old ladies of the family or village. In complication, *dais* are also called for help. They do not like to consult the doctors during pregnancy period and not to take help in the delivery by Doctor or Nursing staff of dispensaries/hospital where these services are available. They only follow the traditional methods of the delivery so generally in complicated case, the expectant mother collapse and in such cases very bit chancc for the survival of infant.

The navalcord or umblicial cord of the infant, cut with a sharp knifc of a daggcr, and is burried in a hole near the house. The naval cord is generally hurried by the uncle of the infant. The mother in law of the women, unless she lives in the same house, usually arrives some time after the birth of the baby. The birth of the male child is announced by acting a *Thali* (Metal plate), and in case of female, is announced by beating a *supra* (Winnowing fan). This custom, indicates that the status of male child is superior the female *i.e.* son is superior than daughter.

The mother is confined to bed for some time i.e. about 2 to 3 weeks after the childs birth, this period considered the complete rest period or recovery period for the mother. During the confinement period the family members look after the mother and infant and other children if they have any.

On the occasion of child birth, parents feel very pleasure, but other family members also feel pleasure. During first delivery the expectant mother feels pleasure, but also feels abnormal and fear with danger of the delivery.

Diet of the Mother

In Bhil society after delivery the mother is keep on the special liquids, locally known as *Kada* is given 3–4 times daily. This Kada is prepared by the helps. It is believed that all the impurities or damages in the body of mother will be required by this mixture, in Kada generally *Gur* (Jaggery) is mixed for changing the taste of it.

After 3–4 days of the delivery the mother is given food once in a day upto a week. The mother is given nutritious food during this period and upto 15–20 days after the delivery. The main contents of these food are of excess fat, Gum, Azama and some herbs. They believe that such type of food will be helpful in recovering the loss of energy and good for health. Such type of food may also helps in increasing the mothers milk and maintain the good quality of milk, so the infant may keep healthy.

After 15–20 days the mother takes normal diet as the other family members. The confinement period ranges from 7 days to one month, but generally it is observed for three weeks.

Rituals on Child Birth

The first ritual after the child birth is *Suraj Pujan*. The *Suraj Pujan* is generally observed after the births 7th or 9th days. On that day purifictory bath is given to mother and child both, before bath the infant and mother are given with a *Peethe i.e.* a paste of oil, turmeric and wheat or barley flour. After bath the mother & child wear new cloths. For the *Suraj Pujan* mother is seated on the *Patta* (Wooden Plate form) facing towards sun *i.e.* east, and the infant is put in her lap. A lighted Deepak (earthen lamp), some fire on the till locally known as Kelu, is placed in front of the mother. A coconut is broken, and some of its small pieces along with some Ghee is put on the fire placed on *Kelu*. Then in some families child's father pour some liquor near the fire. It is supposed that all these offerings are for the clan goddess, *Bheru* and for the chief Bhil deity. On this ceremony Gugari (Boild wheat or maize) and Gur (Jaggery) are distributed to all the members present at that time and also distributed to the neighbourers. This ceremony is generally attended by relatives of both the sides, neighbours. On that day ladies also song on the day of *Suraj Pujan*. Parents of mother of infant and Bhua (father's sister) bring cloths to the mother and child and other relatives and neighbours also give some gift to infant according to their status.

Few days after *Suraj Pujan*, namining ceremony is observed. Generally the name is given by the fathers sister, but in some places Pandit (Brahmin) also named the infant according to stars. Father's sister generally gives the name of infant according to the birthday, name of month, Hindi Date, name of weeks days, on the name of flowers etc. *e.g.* in case of *boys soma* (Birth on Monday), *Puna* (Birth on full moon day), *Duja* (Second), *Gulab* (Flower), *Nara* (Tiger), Phulia (Flower), etc, and in case of girls *somli* (birth on monday), *Puni* or *Punam* (birth on full moon day), *champa* (Flower), *Duji* (Second), etc.

The next birth ritual is celebrated on the occasion of Holi festival. This is known as *Dundh.* On this occasion Bhua (father's sister), Aunt (brother's wife) bring presents of clothes and ornaments for the infant and its parents. All persons of the village gives blessings to the infant. They are entertained by the parents of the infant.

The last social ceremony of the infants is *Mundan.* The boy or the girl's hair are cut down in the age of completion of first, third of fifth year. The hair cutting ceremony is observed in presence of their Diety or Bheru, on this occasion feast is organised, the nearest relatives and neighbours gives presented to the infant according to their economic condition.

Marital Status

The Marital status of the respondenty of the family is detailed in the Table 3.1.

Table 3.1: Martial Status of the Respondents

(Number)

S.No.	Marital Age (Years) (Age group)	Lakarwas	Dheekli	Total District
1.	10–15	4	9	13
2.	15–20	19	16	35
3.	20–25	2	–	2
	Total	25	25	50

The Table 3.1 reveals that out of 50 females, 35 were married in the age group of 15–20 years *i.e.* 70 per cent women married in the middle age group. 13 females *i.e.* 26 per cent were married in 10–15 years age, while only 2 or 4 per cent in the age group of 20–25 years.

In Lakarwas village 76 per cent females were married in the age group 15–20, while 64 per cent in Dheekli village. In first group *i.e.* 10–15 years in Lakarwas only 16 per cent were married, while a high percentage *i.e.* 36 per cent married in Dheekli. In the third age group 4 per cent were married in Lakarwas while, none of them in Dheekli. Not a single case was observed in the age group above 25 years.

Age at marriage is an important aspect of fertility. Infant marriage, which is so wide spread among Hindus, but is not observed in Bhil community. In Bhils marriage takes place some years after the girls has reached puberty. From the Table 3.1 we can say that most of the Bhil marriages takes place between the ages of 15–20 years.

In case of early marriage, the pregnancy will be in early age. In early marriage the child born are generally malnutrited and rate of fertility was observed more in comparison to late marriage. The infant mortality rate was observed higher in case of early marriages.

Age at First Inception

The age at first inception is also very important feature which plays a crucial role in fertility. When first inception occurs in early age than mortality will be high, because malnutrition of infants will exists there. It was also observed that in the early age inception, the fertility and mortality rate also increases.

The Table 3.2 indicates the age at first inception of the respondents.

The Table 3.2 revelas that out of 50 females 37 *i.e.* 70 per cent got first inception in the age group of 15–20 years. It observed the general age of first inception was 19 to 20 years of age. 9 females *i.e.* 18 per cent were first pregnant in the age group 20–25 years, and 9 *i.e.* 6 per cent in 25–30 years age group, while only one or 2 per cent were in the age group above 30 years.

Table 3.2: Age at First Inception

(Number)

Sl. No.	Age at first inception (Year)	Lakarwas	Dheekli	Total (District)
1.	15–20	16	21	37
2.	20–25	5	4	9
3.	25–30	3	–	3
4.	Above 30	1	–	1
	Total	25	25	50

In Lakarwas the 16 females *i.e.* 64 per cent female were first time pregnant in the age group 15–20 years, while in Dheekli 21 females *i.e.* 84 per cent. The percentage very high in Dheekli in comparison to Lakarwas village in the age group 15–20 years. In middle age group the number were all most equal. In Lakarwas above 25 years age 4 females *i.e.* 16 per cent got first pregnancy, while in Dheekli not a single case was observed.

Hence we can say that the general age of first inception lies between the age-group 15–20 years or the age is 19–20 years was observed.

Fertality and Mortality

The fertility and mortality in both villages of the respondent families are detailed below in the Table 3.3.

Table 3.3: Sex–wise Fertality and Mortality

(Number)

Sl. No.	Name of Village	Total Number of Inceptions	Total No. of Birth sex-wise			No. of child died			No of alive child		
			Male	Female	Total	Male	Female	Total	Male	Female	Total
1.	Lakarwas	92	50	42	92	15	11	26	35	31	66
2.	Dheekli	78	38	40	78	11	9	20	27	31	58
3.	Total (District)	170	88	82	170	26	20	46	62	62	124

The Table 3.3 reveals that out of 170 child, 124 got alive *i.e.* 72.94 per cent infants alive. It shows that the mortality were 46 or 27.06 per cent.

The percentage of male child was higher in comparison to female child *i.e.* 51.76 per cent male child took birth, while females were 48.24 per cent, out of 27.06 per cent deaths of infants, males were 15.20 and females 11.77 per cent *i.e.* the mortality of male child is higher in comparison to famale child. Hence from the Table 4.3 we can say that the male mortality is about 25 per cent higher in comparison to female child.

In Lakarwas out of 172 child, 92 were took birth *i.e.* 54 per cent, while 78 or 45.88 per cent in Dheekli, hence 20 per cent excess child took birth in Lakarwas in comparison to Dheekli.

In both the villages the male child mortality was higher in comparison to female child. It was also observed that in both the villages the alive famale child percentage is the same.

The age-wise and village-wise infant mortality is detailed in the Table 3.4.

From the Table 3.4 the highest mortality were 34.78 per cent in age group 6–12 months, the mortaility in male and female is equal in this group *i.e.* 17.39 per cent. Second stands the age group 0–1 month, in this group the mortality was 30.43 per cent, the percentage of male mortality is just double in this group *i.e.* male mortality were 19.57 per cent and female mortality were 10.86 per cent.

13.05 per cent mortality were observed in the age group 3–6 month, in this age group the male mortality was 8–70 per cent while female mortality were 2–35 per cent. In other words we can say that in this group male mortality is four times higher than famale. 8.70 per cent mortality were observed in the age group 12–18 months, in this age group male and famale child mortality, is same, 6.52 per cent mortality were observed in the age group 1–3 months, in this group the male child mortality is just double to the female child *i.e.* male 4.35 and

Table 3.4: Sex-wise and Age-wise Mortality

(Number)

Sl. No.	Name of Village	0–1 month			1–3 month			3–6 month			6–12 month			12–18 month			18–24 month			24 month 4 years			Total		
		M	F	T	M	F	T	M	F	T	M	F	T	M	F	T	M	F	T	M	F	T	M	F	T
1.	Lakarwas	6	6	10	–	–	–	2	1	3	5	4	9	1	2	3	–	–	–	1	–	1	15	11	26
2.	Dheekli	3	1	4	2	1	3	2	1	3	3	4	9	1	–	1	–	1	1	–	1	1	11	9	20
	Total (District)	9	5	14	2	1	3	4	2	6	8	8	16	2	2	4	–	1	1	1	1	2	26	20	46

famale 2.17 per cent. 4.35 per cent mortality were observed in the age group 24 months to 4 years in this group the male and female child mortality were equal *i.e.* 2.17 per cent. The lowest mortality were observed in the age group 18–24 months *i.e.* 2.17 per cent, not a single male mortality were observed in this group.

The mortality were higher in the village Lakarwas in comparison to Dheekli the main cause of mortality were lack of awareness and medical facilities at the villages *i.e.* most of the infants mortality in both the villages caused due to fever, cholera and other unidentified diseases.

The age–wise and sex–wise population of alive child is detailed in the Table 3.5.

Table 3.5: Sex-wise Population of Alive Child

(Number)

Sl. No.	Age-group (Year)	Population		
		Male	Female	Total
1.	0–4	29	34	63
2.	4–9	25	15	40
3.	9–16	8	13	21
	Total (District)	62	62	124

The above Table 3.5 reveals that the male and female child ratio is same in the district as a whole. More than 50 per cent infants covered in the age group 0–4 years, while 32.26 per cent in the age group 4–9 years and rest 16.98 per cent in the age group 9–16 years.

Out of 63 infants 29 age male *i.e.* 46.03 per cent, while females are 34 *i.e.* 53.97 per cent. Hence we can say that in the infant age group female child population is about eight per cent higher in comparison to male child.

From the Table 3.5 we can say that infants dominate in the child group. In infants group the females dominate in comparison to a males. Hence the infants plays an important role in the family and they needs more attention and care by the parents specially from the mother side.

Nutrition

The nutrition of infant plays an important role in the child rearing practices. In rural areas infants is generally fed by breast up to the age of one and a half year or about two years. During the breast feeding the infants are supplemented by other food after attaining the age of 6 months or more than that. Generally after 2 years the infants is given normal food througout the whole infency period *i.e.* upto the age of 4. years. The Nutritional practices adopted in Bhil society is detailed below.

Breast Feeding

Human milk is ideal food for the infant's. It is very easily digestable for them and have all the components and enough amount of water. It has the economic advance of passing direct from producer to consumer. The incidence of infection and gastrointestinal up sets is significantly less in breast feeding in comparison to artificial feeding by bottle and other methods.

In Bhil women or mothers, breast feeding is very much popular. This practice of breast feeding is generally adopted, because they can not afford artificial feeding practices due to their poor economic condition. In other words we can say that their poor economic condition is useful for the infants. In Bhil society the breast feeding duration is very long, in some cases breast feeding goes up to $2^{1/2}$ years of the child age.

The comfort enjoyed by the infant in contact with a soft breast instead of hard bottle, and the confidence gained by the mother in supplying the infant's needs herself, are factors in the successful rearing of infants which is difficult. Assess economically, by but may be assumed to have real importance. The mother feed their infants, when ever they cry, even in odd hours also. They feel that, it is very convenient method of feeding the infant and have no problem in feeding.

In Bhil society the feeding is not given just after the birth, while it should be given immediately after the birth, because at that time the milk is rich in colostrum, which provides immunity against gastro interstinal and respiratory infections and allergies. The details regarding breast feeding after the birth are given in Table 3.6.

Table 3.6: Starting of Breast Feeding

(Number)

Sl. No.	Duration of breast feeding (In days)	Name of village		Total (District)
		Lakarwas	Dheekli	
1.	Immediately after birth	–	3	3
2.	After 3 days	24	20	44
3.	After seven days	1	2	3
	Total	25	25	50

The above Table 3.6 reveals that out of 50 mothers 44 feed their infant after 3 days of delivery *i.e.* 88 per cent, while 3 mother feed their infant immediately after birth *i.e.* 6 per cent and rest 3 or 6 per cent feed their infant after 7 days of birth.

In Lakarwas village not a single mother feed their infant immediately after birth. In this village 96 per cent mothers feed their infant after three days of delivery and 4 per cent mothers feed their infant after seven days. In Bhils after the birth of child is given a *Kada* made of some herbals to the infant, it is locally known as *Gulla* till the breast feeding starts.

In Dheekli 12 per cent mother feed their infant immediately after the birth, 80 per cent mother feed after the three days of delivery, while 8 per cent feed after seven days. They also give *Gulla* till the breast feeding starts.

The reason of late feeding after 7 days is non availability of breast milk. The reason after three days feeding is tradition and have no cause after it. They feel that after three days, feeding is better for the health of the child. They believe that first two days milk is not good for the child.

The duration of breast feeding varies from family to family and also keeping in view the health of the infants. The details regarding duration of breast feeding is given in Table 3.7.

Table 3.7: Duration of Breast Feeding

(Number)

Sl. No.	Duration of Breast (In months)	Name of village		Total (District)
		Lakarwas	Dheekli	
1.	6–12 Month	2	–	2
2.	12–18 month	9	6	15
3.	18–24 month	11	13	24
4.	24 month above	3	6	9
	Total	25	25	50

The above Table 3.7 reveals that out of 50 mothers, a maximum number 24 *i.e.* 48 per cent feed their infant upto the age group 18–24 months. It follows 15 *i.e.* 30 per cent by the group 12–18 months, while 9 or 18 per cent mother feed their infants more than 24 months of age, rest 2 *i.e.* 4 per cent mothers feed their infants upto 6–12 month. The reason for short time feeding is non-availability of milk. In both the, villages, not a single mother feed their infant less than 6 months.

In both the villages the prevalent group of breast feeding is 18–24 months, age while Dheekli 12–18 months and above 24 months age group have same number *i.e.* same per cent of infant, not a single infant in the age group 6–12 month, while in Lakarwas the second group is 12–18 months infants, and above 24 month age group has third position. The lowest group in Lakarwas is 6–12 months. Hence we can say that every mother feed their infant upto minimum of more than six months.

Supplementary Food

The supplementary food is very essential for the infants, when they grew or attain the age after 6 months the quantity of breast milk reduces and the hunger of infant increases. So the breast milk is not sufficient for the infant and can not feed properly without supplementation. If supplementation is not given, the infant will cry and fell ill and will be in the grip of malnutrition and got pale. Hence supplementary food is necessary after the age of 6 months.

In Urban areas the supplementary food is started after 3 or 4 months age of infants, because the mothers do not like to feed the infant by breast. They generally replace breast. Feeding by bottle feeding after the age of 3 or 4 months age of the infants, at mean time, other liquid food like fruit juices are also given and generally after the age of six months baby foods, which canned in tins are given with bottle feeding or feeding by paste manner. The bottle feeding is generally by animal milk, and if it is not available, than canned powder milk is used. In urban areas no discreation of animal milk can be seen, they give whatever type of milk may be.

In rural areas the supplementary food is given in late age, because generally they can not afford very costly food products. The generally give diluted animal milk, diluted curd locally known as Chach or pridge *i.e.* Dalia (Made of grind wheat).

In Bhil society the supplementation of nutrition exists. In the supplementary food they generally provide goat milk, because Bhils generally have goats and they also believe that goats milk is easily digestable and need not any dilution. Some families those who have cow or buffalow, also supplemented by them, but the second preference is given to the cow's milk. The cow milk is not given directly, it is diluted upto 50 per cent according to the age of the infant. The buffallow milk is supplemented or given when no other type of animal milk is available, it is believed that buffalow milk is not easily digestable. The buffalow milk is diluted upto 100 per cent according to the age of the infant.

In Lakarwas out of 25 respondent mothers, 24 supplement the infant food by goat milk, while 8 mothers also use cow milk, only one mother gives buffalow milk. In Dheekli village 21 mothers feed their infants by goat milk, while a mothers also use cow milk, 4 mothers exclusively supplement their infant by cow milk, not a single mother used buffalow milk in this village.

In both the villages bottle feeding practice was not observed. They feed their infant with Katori (Metal bowl) and spoon, if he can not take it directly. In case of some elder infant metal tumbler (Glass) is used for the milk feeding. The Bhils do not use powder milk, canned baby foods, fruit juice and other solid or semi solid foods, because of poor economic condition and they can not get it easily. So they supplement the other solid or semi-solid food whatever they eat in routine (normal) diet is given to the infant.

They supplement their infant by *Dalia* (made of grind wheat), *Rab* (Maize flour is backed with diluted curd *i.e. chach*), and Roti. Roti is generally not given directly, it is given by mixing it very well in milk or chach or curd. Some families who afford also give boiled rice to the infant, but the cases are very rare, rice is not given daily.

The starting of supplementary food during breast feeding, the age-wise distribution is given in the Table 4.8.

Table 3.8: Time Schedule of Supplementary Nutrition

(Number)

Sl. No.	Age group (In month)	Name of village		Total (District)
		Lakarwas	Dheekli	
1.	0–6	2	4	6
2.	6–12	23	20	43
3.	12–18	–	1	1
	Total	25	25	50

The above Table 3.8 revelas that out of 50 respondents mothers, 43 supplement their infant in age group 6–12 month *i.e.* 86 per cent. It was observed the supplementation if generally started after 6 month *i.e.* from the 8th month of the infant. Second group is of the age 0–6 months, in this group mothers feed their infant, the case of early supplementation is due to lack supply of breast milk. Only one mother has started supplementation in the age group 12–18 months. The late supplementation case was observed in Dheekli village. The dominant group in both the villages for supplementation was 6–12 months of age.

In Bhil society the supplementary food given is generally not nutritious, because they are not in a position to afford costly nutritious food and such type of food is not available nearby the villages, so if one want's to feed, he can not feed them. In this manner malnutrition is generally observed in all the respondent families. The children are very lean and thin and underweight.

Weaning

Breast feeding is an ideal food for the infant, but it can not be continued for a long period. Because the quantity of milk reduces when the times passes and hunger of infant increases with the growth. So breast feeding must be stopped after a certain period.

In Bhil society weaning is not started earlier. The breast feeding is carried for a long period. Generally breast feeding is supplemented by other food and the frequency is reduced slowly.

The age-wise distribution of weaning is started given in the Table 3.9

The Table 3.9 reveals that most common weaning age goup liked by the Bhil mothers is 18–24 months. Out 50 mothers, 22 *i.e.* 44 per cent have stated weaning from this age group in both the villages, second stands 12–18 month age group and above 24 months age group in third position, while 6–12 months age group have only one mother in Dheekli village. Hence the weaning is started not before 6 months age of the infant, but generally it is started after completion of $1^{1/2}$ years age of the infant. The long-term feeding also helpful as a contraceptive to the feeding mother.

Table 3.9: Age-wise Districution of Initiation of Weaning

(Number)

S.No.	Age group (In month)	Name of village		Total (District)
		Lakarwas	Dheekli	
1.	6–12	1	–	1
2.	12–18	8	6	14
3.	18–24	9	13	22
4.	above 24	7	6	13
	Total	25	25	50

The mode of weaning differs from family to family, but the most prevalent method used by the respondent Bhil mothers are detailed in the Table 3.10.

Table 3.10: Mode of Weaning

(Number)

S.No.	Name of Village	Mode of weaning		Supple-mentary food and med. both	Total
		by supple-mentary food	by medi-cines		
1.	Lakarwas	8	8	9	25
2.	Dheekli	14	10	1	25
	Total	22	18	10	50

The above Table 3.10 reveals that the most popular method is supplementary food. During the weaning period the quantity of supplementary food increases and the frequency of breast feeding reduces. First of all the day time feeding frequency reduced and ultimately day time breast feeding stopped, then nigh feeding stops. If the supplementation method fails then the mothers use the last resort by applying medicines on the nipple. The most common medicine applied on nipple is *Neem leaves paste*. Due to the bitter taste, infant do not like to touch the nipple. Hence this last resort is mot effective method.

Regular (Routine) Diet

Regular or Routine diet of the infant is started after the breast feeding or the completion of weaning. Generally in regular diet the supplementary diet converts into routine diet. In routine diet liquid food is also given, but the quantity of solid and semi-solid food increased by the gaining in age of the infant. In this manner the liquid diet is replaced slowly by the semi-solid and solid food products.

In both the villages the infants are generally given milk of goat or cow which ever is easily available. In some families buffalow milk is also given. Buffalow milk is given not pure, but it is diluted upto 100 per cent according the age group, because it is believed that this milk is heavy and not digestable easily.

The infants are given Dalia, Rab, boiled rice and Roti (Bread). The Rab and bread (Roti) is given daily, while rice and Dalia are given casually. Casually boiled rice is mixed with milk and sugar are given to the infant, this dish is known as Kheer. Roti is generally crushed in milk or Chach. So the infant can eat it easily. Casually the Roti is mixed with dal also. The crushed Roti is easily digestable.

The Bhils casually give their infants biscuits also. So the regular diet of the infants is similar to the other family members.

Difference between the Diet of Male and Female

In Bhil society the male and female are given equal importance in the family, because she also plays an important role in the economic field. During the observation in Lakarwas 23 families have no discrimination *i.e.* 92 per cent in the diet of male and female issue, while 2 families *i.e.* 8 per cent observe discrimination. They feed males first, then the rest food is given to the females, hence the quality of food will remain same, but quantity may be insufficient. In Dheekli village no such type of discrimination was observed. They treat male and female equally.

Sufficiency of Food

Food must be sufficient for every member of the family to keep them healthy. In the Bhil society, due to economic constraints some families do not get enough food. They only get food for survival. So in this manner most of the families are malnutrited. The availability of food and reasons for non-availability detailed in the Table 3.11.

Table 3.11: Availability of Food

Sl.No.	Name of the village	Availability of Reasons fon non-availability				
		Food			Economic constant (Poverty)	non availability of food products
		Yes	No	Total		
1.	Lakarwas	11	14	25	10	4
2.	Dheekli	16	9	25	9	–
	Total (District)	27	23	50	19	4

The Table 3.11 reveals that out of 50 families, 27 familes get sufficient food, *i.e.* 54 per cent, while rest 23 *i.e.* 46 per cent do not get sufficient food for survival. In Lakarwas more than 50 per cent families do not get sufficient food, while in Dheekli 64 per cent families get sufficient food. The main reason of non-availability of food products is poverty or economic constraint, while non-availability means the desired food products are not available at the village.

Hence poverty is main hurdle in the sufficiency of food so they are mostly malnutriated.

Food Habits

Food habits means the duration and the food products given to the infant. If the infant will be given food without any restrictions, the infant will be fell ill. So some restrictions, the infant will be fell ill. So some restrictions are very necessary to check the diet. This procedure is called food habits.

The details of duration *i.e.* gap between the diet and the frequency of diet of infants detailed in the Table 3.12.

Table 3.12: Frequency of Diet

(Number)

Sl. No.	Name of village	Frequency (in no.)				Duration (Gap in hours)			
		2	3	4	more than 4 times	3–4	4–5	5–6	more than 6
1.	Lakarwas	–	14	9	1	3	15	4	2
2.	Dheekli	1	11	12	1	4	17	3	1
	Total (District)	1	25	21	2	7	32	7	3

The Table 3.12 reveals that out 50 families, 25 families provides food thrice daily *i.e.* 50 per cent, 21 *i.e.* 44 per cent families provide food four time daily to their infants, while only one family feed their infant once in a day, 2 families provides more than 4 times. The case of single time feeding in due to the infant is very young.

If we consider the duration or interval of feeding, maximum infants are needed by the families within the interval of 4–5 hours. Hence the duration of feeding and frequency is quite sufficient and hygienic.

Learning Habits

After goining the age of one year, drastic change occurs in the nature of infant. The infant tries to crawling, pronouncing some words *i.e.* tries to speak, but have no sense of toilet habits. At that time parents are required to pay more attention

Table 3.13: Learning Habits and Duration

(Number)

Sl. No.	Name of village	No. of H.H's	Walking (in months)					Speaking (in months)					Toilet		Reading	
			6-9	9-12	12-15	15-18	18-24	12-15	15-18	18-24	24+	N.A.	18-24	24+	24+	N.A.
1.	Lakarwas	25	–	10	6	5	1	5	11	5	1	3	16	6	6	–
2.	Dheekli	25	4	4	4	8	3	1	4	14	22	3	4	18	–	–
	Total	50	4	14	10	13	4	6	15	19	23	6	20	24	–	–

on infants. In Bhil society the parents are illiterate and have no time to devote on the infants, but mothers and elder children tries to attend the infants of the family. They also tries to trained the infants, whenever they get time according to their understandings.

The parents do no impacted any training by their elders about the child rearing practices. They only flow what their elders do previously. Hence they observe the traditional method or procedure of socializing their infants. The details of learning habits or training habits imputed by the parents are detailed in the Table 3.13.

From the Table 3.13 reveals that most of the children walking in the age-group 9–12 months, second groups fallows 15–18 months age group. Most of the children speaks in the age-group more than 24 months, follows the age-group 18–24 months. Toilet training is imparted generally after 2 years *i.e.* 24 months age group follows it. Education is imparted only 6 families in Lakarwas village.

General Activities

In every family some general habits are formed by the infants. Regarding such type of daily habits, parents guide them and tries that the infants should obey them strictly. By these habits they will be considered a good child. These habits are good for health and hygiene also.

So, during the observation in Bhil society, these training or habits are formed by the parents. The answers is in Yes or No. The details of these are given in the Table 3.14.

The Table 3.14 reveals that sleeping in time and getup every day in time was observed about 50 per cent families, while behavioural training and respect to elders were reached by more than 50 per cent parents. The educational training *i.e.* reading and writing were not learnt by most of the parents, *i.e.* about 90 per cent do pay any attention regarding this matter. Other toilet and sanitation teaching are also imparted by more than 50 per cent parents. Hence in the manner the parents try to teach or educate their infants to help in socialize them.

Table 3.14: Training to Infants

(Number)

Sl. No.	Name of Activities	Name of village				Total (District)	
		Lakarwas		Dheekli			
		Yes	No	Yes	No	Yes	No
1.	To sleep and getup every day in fixed time	8	14	14	9	22	23
2.	Washes every day after getup	14	8	20	3	34	11
3.	Bathing	16	6	11	12	27	18
4.	To wear clean clothes	12	10	13	10	25	20
5.	To clean teeth	13	9	18	5	31	14
6.	To take meals at fixed time	11	11	16	7	27	18
7.	Play	5	17	5	18	10	35
8.	Behavioural training and respect to elders	6	16	19	4	25	20
9.	Reading and writing	3	19	1	22	4	40

Child Care during Working Hours

During working hours parents goes on field or on the labour. Generally parents keep their infants with them. Out of 50 families, 41 families *i.e.* 82 per cent families keeps their kids with them. In six families *i.e.* 12 per cent infants are looked after by the elder children, while in three families the infants are looked after by the grand mother. The situation is same in both the villages. The parents feed their infants on the work side when they get free or the child cries. In other words during the working hours the infants are not looked after properly by the parents.

Recreation

Recreation is very essential for the regular growth of the infants. Sports *i.e.* playing of infants with toys also impart them educational training as well as helpful in developing the understanding of the child.

Due to the poor economic condition the Bhil families are not in a position to provide toys to their infants. The details of sources of recreation are given in the Table 3.15.

Table 3.15: Availability and Sources of Recreation

(Number)

Sl.No.	Name of village	Availability of toys			If 'yes' Nature of		
		Yes	No	Total	Mud	Wooden	Plastic
1.	Lakarwas	8	17	25	1	1	6
2.	Dheekli	9	16	25	–	4	8
	Total (District)	17	33	50	1	5	14

The above Table 3.15 reveals that only 34 per cent families have toys made of mud, wood and plastic, while 66 per cent no toys due to poor economic condition. The situation in both the villages are the same.

Case Material

Case-I

The first case was observed of Smt. Tulsi Bai W/O Parta Ji of Lakarwas. She was married in the age of 16 and was got pregnant after one year of the marriage *i.e.* the first conception was in the 17 year age. The main occupation of the family is agriculture as well as labour. Both the adult member *i.e.* husband and wife goes on work. At the time of survey Tulsi Bai was of 22 years age. She is illiterate.

The economic condition of this family can not say good. The average monthly income of both the earners are about Rs. 600. They have two bighas of irrigated land, but they have not their own well. They have one pair of bullock and 10 goats.

This family have two infants one male and one female. The age of male child is 5 years and female is of about 2 years. One male child died in this family, within a week after the delivery due to unidentified disease. In this family all the deliveries take place at home. The infants of the family are very weak, this family has knowledge about the immunitation, both the child have immenised and given D.P.T., Khasra and Polio Vaccine.

Tulsi was rearing their infants by the traditional manner. She has started breast feeding after three days of delivery and feed the child upto 20 months age. She has started weaning after 20 months of age attained by the infant. She has started supplementary food after 8 months age of the infant. The weaning is started by increasing the quantity of supplementary food.

The supplementary food given by her are goat milk, Dalia (Porridge) Rab and Roti, sometimes she give boiled rice. The routine diet of the infant given by her is same as they eat in normal days *i.e.* goat milk, Rab, Dalia, Roti, Dal etc. She feed their infants generally thrice daily, within the interval of about 6 hours. The food given to infants is sufficient for their needs. Their infants have no sources of recreation *i.e.* toys due to economic constraints. She keep their infants with them during the working hours. Her infants started walking in the age of 12 months, speaking in about 16 months age and Toilet training after the age of 24 months. She has given behavioural training and given some essential training regarding daily routine. Hence she is rearing their infants in a good manner, in which she can afford.

Case-II

Smt Dali Bai W/O Roda Ji of Lakarwas was married in the age of 23 years. At the time of interview she has about 46 years. She got pregnant in late age, the firsts inception was in the age of 34 years. The main occupation of this family is agriculture as well as labour. Of Both the adult members goes on work. She is also illiterate.

The economic condition of the family is better in comparison to case–I. The average monthly income of both the earners are about Rs 1,000. They have 5 Bighas barron land. They have only one goat on the name of live-stock.

This family have 3 male child and one female child, the age of male children are 8, 5, years and youngest child is of 6 months and famale is of 12 years. In this family a large number of infants died *i.e.* 3 males and 3 femals from the age 15 days to $1^{1/2}$ year due to unidentified disease. In this family all deliveries took place at home. They have not immunised their infants due to non-availability of health services.

Dali Bai is rearing their infants in traditional manner. She has also started breast feeding after three days of delivery and feed the infants upto the age of $1^{1/2}$ year. In similar manner she has also started weaning after $1^{1/2}$ year of age attained by the infants. She has started supplementary food after 8 months age of the infant. The weaning has been stated by increasing the quantity of supplementary food and applying Neem paste on the nipples. The supplementary food given by her are goat milk, Dalia, Rab and Roti, some time she also give boiled rice. The routine diet of the infants given by her is same as they eat during the supplementation *i.e.* goat milk, Rab, Roti, Dalia, Rice etc. She feed their infants thrice daily, within the interval of about 4–5 hours. The food given to infants is sufficient for their needs. The infants have no sources of recreation *i.e.* toys due to economic constraints. During the working hours the infants are looked after by the elder children. Their infants started walking in the age of 12 month, speaking in about 15 month age and Toilet training after the age of 30 months. She has given no training to children, they believe that infants learn all the habits by their-self to looking others.

Case-III

Smt. Raju Bai W/O Manna ji of Lakarwas was married in the age of 18 years. At the time of interview she was about 39 years. She got pregnant after the two years of marriage *i.e.* in the age of 20 years.

This family has no land, the main occupation of this family is labour. The monthly income of all the earning members reaches about Rs. 800/–. On the name of live-stock they have four goats.

This family have 4 alive children out of them 2 elders are female of the age 10 and 12 years and rest 2 are male child having the age 4 year and 3 years. In this family one male child died within a week of the birth, due to some unidentified diseases.

The condition of all children including infants are very poor. The children are very lean and thin.

Raju Bai is also rearing their infants in traditional manner. She has also started breast feeding after three days of birth of the infant and feet up to the age of 2 years. The supplementary food is started after 6 months age of the infant. The weaning has been started by her applying Neem paste on the Nipples. The supplementary food given by her are goat milk, Dalia, Rab and Roti. In regular diet she feed their infant thrice daily, within the interval of about 6–8 hours. In the regular diet she gives them Dalia, Rab, Roti and milk. The food given to infants is insufficient according to their needs. The infants have no sources of recreation *i.e.* toys due to economic constraints. During working hours the infants are looked after by the grand-mother of the infants. Her infants started walking and speaking in the age of $1^1/_2$ year and toilet training after the age of 24 months. She has not given any training to the children due to non-awareness of rearing practices. The infants of this family were not immunised due to lack of knowledge and non-availability of health services. Hence in this family the infants were malnutriated and have hand to mouth.

Case-IV

Smt. Dali Bai W/O Kana ji of Dheelbi was married in the age of 15 years. At the time of interview she was about 30 years. She got pregnant after three years of marriage *i.e.* in the age of 18 years. The main occupation of this family is agriculture of both the adults. She is also illiterate.

The economic condition of this family can not say good. The average monthly income of both the earners are about Rs. 500. They have two bighas of irrigated land, but have not their own source of irrigation. This family have not a single livestock.

This family has four alive children 3 females and one male, the age of females are 12, 7 and 3 years, while male is of only 5 months age. One male child died in the family after the birth of 5 month due to unidentified disease. All the infants have been immunised by small pox., D.P.T. and given Polio vaccine.

Dali Bai is rearing their infants by the traditional manner. She has started breast feeding after three days of delivery and feed the infant upto 14 month age. She has started weaning after $1^{1/2}$ years of age attained by the infant. She has started supplementary food after 6 months age of the infant. The weaning is started after the age of $1^{1/2}$ year increasing the quantity of supplementary food. The supplementary food given by her are goat and cow milk, Dalia, Rab and Roti. The routine diet of the infant given by her is same as they eat in normal days *i.e.* Milk Rab, Roti, Dal etc. She feed their infant generally four times daily, within the interval of about 4–5 hours. The food given to infants is generally sufficient according to their needs. The infant have few toys made of wood and plastic.

During the working hours the infants are looked after by the old family members like grand father and grand mother. Her infants started walking in the age of $1^{1/2}$ year, speaking in the age of 2 years and toilet training after the the age of

$2^1/_2$ years. She has give behavioural training and also imparted some essential training regarding daily routine. Hence she is rearing their infants in a good manner in which she can manage easily.

Case-V

Smt. Janki Bai W/O Amba Lal of Dheekli was married in the age of 15 years at the time of interview she was about 25 years. She got pregnant after three year of marriage *i.e.* the age of 18 years. The main occupation of this family is agriculture as well as labour of both the earners. She is also illiterate.

The economic condition of this family is better in comparison to case IV *i.e.* from Dali Bai. The average monthly income of both the earners are about Rs. 600. They have one bigha of irrigated land, but have no source of their own irrigation. This family have one cow, 2 bullocks and 2 goat.

This family has two alive children one female of 3 years and one male of one year. In this family a large a number of infants died *i.e.* 4 males in the age group of 1, 2, 3 and 6 months after the birth due to unidentified diseases. The infants of this family have been immunised *i.e.* by D.P.T. and Polio Vaccine.

Janki Bai is rearing their infants in traditional manner. She has started breast feeding just after the birth of the infant. The breast feeding started just after the birth is very good for the infant health. Breast feeding is given by her upto the age of $2^{1/2}$ years. She has started supplementary food after the age of 6 months. The weaning is started after the age of $2^{1/2}$ years by increasing the quantity of supplementary food. The supplementary food given by her are diluted cow milk, Rab and Roti. The routine diet of the infant given by her is same as they eat in normal days *i.e.* Milk, Roti, Dalia and Rab, etc. She feed their infant generally four times daily within the interval of about 4–5 hours. The food given to infant is not enough because of economic constraint. The infants have no source of recreation *i.e.* toys, the main reason for it is poverty.

During the working hours parents keep their infants with them.

Her infants started walking in the age of 9 months, speaking in the age of 2 years and Toilet training after the age of $2^1/_2$ years. She has imparted behavioural training and also imparted some essential training regarding daily routine.

Case-VI

Smt. Ratni Bai W/O Tulsi Ram was married in the age of 16 years and get pregnant after the two years of marriage *i.e.* in 18 years age. At the time of interview she was 25 years old.

The economic condition of this family can not say good. This family has 2 bighas irrigated land, but have not their own source of irrigation. They have a pair of bullock on the name of live-stock.

This family has 3 alive children, 2 female of the age 6 and 3 years and one male of 4 months. In this family one female child died after the birth of one year due to unidentified disease. The infants of this family are also immunised by D.P.T. and Polio Vaccine.

Ratni Bai is also rearing their infants in traditional manner. She has started breast feeding just after the birth and feed their infants upto the age of 2 years. She has started supplementary food after 6 months age of the infant. The weaning is started after the age of 2 years by increasing the quantity of supplementary food. The supplementary food given by her are diluted cow milk, Rab and Roti. The routine diet of the infant is similar to the supplementary food *i.e.* the routine diet they take normally is Milk, Roti, Rab, Dal etc. She feed their infants generally four times daily, within the gap of about 4–5 hours. The food given to the infants are not enough due to economic constraints. The infants of the family have not a single toy, because they can not afford it due to poverty. During the working hours they keep infants with them. Her infants started walking in the age of $1^{1/2}$ year, speaking in the age of 2 year and Toilet training after the age of 3 years. She has in pasted behavioural training and also imparted some essential training regarding daily routine nature like sanitation bathing, early rise and go to bed in time etc.

Hence in Bhil society the child rearing practices are very much different to the other groups of the society. They generally rear their infants by what the sources available according to their status. They do not borrow anything for their infants. They feed their infants in a routine manner and not manage any thing special for them. So we can say that the rearing practices in the Bhil societies are very simple. These practices can be seen throughout the region.

The Bhil infants needs a few cloths. In infancy period males *i.e.* boys wears only shirt or Jhabla on the upper portion and upto the age of one year triangular cloth known as *Langoti* is tied with the writ of the infant. After the age of two years, they wear half point, but generally wear no cloth. The females wears Jhabla or Frock upto the age of four years. On the upper portion of the body. In lower portion upto the age of one year Langoti is tied with the wrist of the girl. After the age she wears Chaddi or some wear skirt or Ghaghara and blouse. So the infants in the Bhil society needs very nominal clothes to cover their bodies and have no varieties of cloths. In this manner the infants of this society are rearing in minimal expenditure, but due to non-awareness of the parents, they are ignored unknowingly and they can not reared properly.

Malnutrition exists in every family *i.e.* they feed their childrens according to their abbetite, but they do not know what are the deficiencies exists in infants of what the food stuff actually essential for good health for their infants.

I.O.D.S. (Integrated Child Development Services)

This programme is carried out or complemented by the state government through Mahila Avam Bal Vikas Vibhag, Rajasthan, through the network of *Anganwaris*. By this programme supplementary food is provided to pregnant and lactating mothers along with the infants from 0–6 years of age. During the pregnancy and lactating period, the mother required more energy to feed their infant before birth in womb and after birth by breast feeding. During pregnancy, she requires 300 calories more energy and during first phase of breast feeding *i.e.* upto 0–6 months requires 550 calories, and from 6–12 months requires 400 calories, more energy to maintain the health of the mother; these normals were assessed by I.C.M.R. in 1981.

In rural areas and in urban slum areas, where poor people reside or poverty exists, they are not in a position to afford nutritius food during pregnancy and lactating period. They are also not in a position to feed their infants in a good manner due to economic constraints.

Keeping in view the economic condition of the poors, *Anganwari* services were introduced to help the mother and child. By Anganwaris in rural areas health services are also rendered.

The normals prescribed by the Mahila Avam Bal Vikas Vibhag for the supplementary food during 1990–91 detailed in Table 3.16.

The norms prescribed in the Table 3.16 are very bit. By these normal nobody can be feed properly or supplemented, even the infants.

Both the villages have one Anganwari in each. The Anganwari is located between the village. In general, the expectant and lactating mothers and infants enrolled are non-tribals and scheduled castes, only 2–3 were Bhils.

Bhils lives in halment or Phala's which are far from the village *i.e.* Bhils do not like to reside in the village. Hence they do not send their females and infants in Anganwari. The other reason is that, during Pregnancy and lactacting period women goes on work and have no time to go in the Anganwari, and have no interest to send the infants in Anganwari, because when they send infant, some elder member of family must accompany them.

Table 3.16: Standard Norms of Nasta Distribution

Sl. No.	Name of the Item	For 0–6 years children		For lactating & pregnant women		Name of the Item	Paisa (Per child women)
		Dalia In Paisa	Dalia Gm	Dalia in Paisa	Dalia Gm		
	Local food items					From central assistance	
1.	Wheat	18	80	34	150	Wheat	16
2.	Dal	09	10	18	20	Dal	9
3.	Oil	15	09	15	09	Gur	5
4.	Gur/Salt	05	According to taste	05	According to taste	Oil	10
5.	Transport	02	–	02	–	Salt	1
6.	Fuel	05	–	05	–	Fuel	5
7.	Grinding Charges	01	–	01	–	Grading charges Transport	2 2
	Total	55 Paisa		80 Paisa			50 Paisa

In other words we can say that, Anganwari's are useless for the Bhil society. There is a urgent need to reorganize the structure of Anganwari according to the requirements (needs) of the Bhil tribals. The centres should be opened in Bhil halmets Phalas and the time should be fixed according to the convenience of the families of halmets/Phalas.

Hence the Bhils are not particular about the feeding practices as-well-as health services. They are very careless about the health. They only avail medical facilities when there is a urgent need.

4 Health Process and Child Care

Although growth and development are closely related and both continue from the moment of conception to the point at which adulthood is reached, they are essentially two different processes. Grouth implies increase in size, typically coupled with cell-division and enlargement of protoplasmic and skeletal structure, where as development represents increasing maturation of tissues, organs, or of the whole individual until full, maturity of structure and function is attained. There are wide differences in the rate of growth of different organs and tissues at different stages of development. This is reflected in the changing proportions of the body during, infancy, childhood and adolescence.

For the proper development it is very essential that the infants must be well feeded and quite healthy. The healthy infants will grows in better ways and in future he will be not burden on the family as-well-as on the society.

In preventive medicine, maternal and child health is defined as "the field of work related to the physical, mental and emotional health of women immediately before, during and after child birth and of infants and young children". Health services begins from the time of conception; and therefore the pre-natal, intra-natal and post-natal supervision of mother is included in the services for her. Prenatal services ensure the health of expectant mother, more specifically her nutritional status, is periodically supervised and avoidable complications of pregnancy are prevented or treated. Intranatal services provide skilled care and attention by trained widwives (Dais) during child birth. Postnatal care includes mother and child health services after delivery.

Child health services consciously aim at the prevention of illness among the children and at an early detection and correction of illness when it occurs. Such type of health services are helpful in reducing the infant mortality. Child health development programme now include not only measures for the prevention and care of diseases, but the promotion of vigorous and healthy growth and development of children.

In India ICDS *i.e.* interated child development programme have been introduced throughout all the states in the Urban areas as-well-as in the remote rural areas. Meternal and child health services covers.

(*i*) Regular checking of a child's growth and development through primary health centres.

(*ii*) The education of the mother in various stages of a child development through *Anganwaries*.

(*iii*) Immunisation against communicable diseases through primary health centres and treatment of minor ailments.

(*iv*) Referral to a proper source for any special preventive or curative action.

Awareness about Health Services

Awareness about the health services can be seen in Urban areas in the educated mass. In rural areas awareness about health services are scarce, because the main cause is illiteracy and non-availability of health services in the rural areas. The health services are generally centralized at the panchayat samiti head quarter and most of the primary health centres are situated in the big villages. Other reasons are lack of communication facilities and costly treatments, so the rural masses generally treat their patients whatever available at the spot *i.e.* they generally use the traditional methods and local herbals. They also consults the Bhopas (a priest) and Tantriks.

In tribal society, such type of traditional treatment practice is very common. In Bhil society the mode of treatments, generally observed are traditional, because they are easily available at their helment or village *i.e.* available on the spot and are very economical, so they can easily afford it. The Bhils, generally use the local herbs as the medicines. They also consult Bhopas (a priest) for the treatment. Bhopas generally give Jhada, some ashes and few amount of grain, grain may be wheat or maize. They have blind faith in Bhopa's treatment. Where Ayurvedic dispensaries exist, they also consult the width for their treatment.

The infants are also treated by the above method. The main causes of infant death's were unidentification of diseases, wrong treatment given by the local persons, hence the infant ultimately died in absence of medicines, and proper treatment. The resistance of infants are very much low in comparison to elder children, so due to lack of awareness and in absence of correct diagnosis, they can not be saved at the spot or in the early stage of disease, when it may be curable.

It is very necessary at the village level, some knowledgeable person should be deputed, so he can advise them for their better treatment and about the health services, it is very necessary for their long survival or life.

Mode of Treatment

During the course of field work, the preference of treatment were enquired by the respondents. The details of preference are given in the Table 4.1

The above Table 4.1 reveals that out of 50 families, 41 have given preference to the traditional treatment *i.e.* 82 per cent families likes traditional treatment. The main cause of first preference is that, it is readily available at the spot or nearby their residence or village, while 6 persons *i.e.* 12 per cent have give first prefercence to allopathy and 3 or 6 per cent were given first priority treatment goes to Ayurvedic. Hence we can say easily that, they prefer traditional treatment.

Table 4.1: Preference of Treatment

(Number)

Sl.No.	Name of village	First			Second			Third		
		Trad.	Allo.	Ayur.	Trad.	Allo.	Ayur.	Trad.	Allo.	Ayur.
1.	Lakarwas	20	4	1	2	9	14	3	12	10
2.	Dheekli	21	2	2	1	12	12	3	11	11
	Total (District)	41	6	3	3	21	26	6	23	21

Second most common treatment preferred by the Bhils is Ayurvedic, while allopathy stands on third or last preference. The reason of last preference for allopathy, because it is not readily available and its is very costly.

Health Care

Child healthcare services are rendered by the primary health centres at the nearby villages. The nurses compounders are bound to motivate the villages to immunise their infants as a precautinary measure. In Bhil society the familes are forced to immunise their infants, it was observed that the families do not want to immunise vaccinate their infants, because they feel that this may cause something wrong with the child.

Table 4.2

Sl.No.	Name of village	Immunisatiary vaccination			If "yes" the details are			
		Yes	No	Total	Small pox	D.P.T.	Palio	Nissles
1.	Lakarwas	14	11	25	2	13	12	4
2.	Dheekli	20	5	25	13	19	19	–
	Total (District)	34	16	50	15	32	31	4

Some families believe that their deities will unhappy due the immunisation vaccination.

The Bhil families, who availed these facilities are given in Table 4.2.

The above Table 4.2 reveals that out of 50 families 34 *i.e.* 68 per cent have immunise/vaccinate their infants. By various types of vaccines for small pox, D.P.T., missles and polio.

HYGIENE

5 Perspective of Hygiene

Health means something more than the absence of illness and the presence of illness should not necessarily be taken to mean poor health. Good health means the persons enjoying physical, emotional, mental and social well being. For the good health it is very necessary that the environmental surroundings must be hygienic and pleasant. These factors naturally effect the health of the human being whether it may be child, young or the elder persons. The environmental conditions and sanitation habits also effect the health conditions. If a person is living with good habits and passing his life in good surroundings will naturally enjoy long life and would be free from illness.

According to 1991 census[1] the tribal population of India constitute 67, 758, 380 persons (67, 751, 026 Rural and 5,007,354 Urban) *i.e.* 8.08 per cent of the population, while in Rajasthan the tribal population constitute 5,474,881 persons (5,220,549 Rural and 254,332 Urban) *i.e.* 12.44 per cent of the state population. Hence about 95 per cent tribals reside in the rural areas. They are deprived of the essential health services as well as sanitation awareness. The lack of awareness of sanitation, results a number of infectious diseases *i.e.* the effected person may fell ill or come into the grip of bad effects. Hence the sanitation awareness indirectly effect their health as well as economic status also.

The concept of health varies from individual to individual. The tribals are far removed from modern, scientific and technical advancement. Because of the their traditionalism, illiteracy and backwardness, they are cut-off from the mainstream of national life. They have their own customs, rituals traditions and taboos.

It is a fact that success of health programmes depends upon modification of human behaviour? Since a large number of tribal communities are there with varied socio-cultural traditions, economy and interaction with outside word, the concept of disease and nature of treatment are likely to be different.

Medical sociology, medical Anthropology is comparatively a new development in the country; but same exploratory studies have been made an different facts of tribal hygiene.

Varrior Elwin has shown a great interest in tribal health, while ethnographic studies have been carried out by S.C. Roy, D.N. Majumdar and others, some data on tribal health are also available. Most of the studies made on tribal groups indicated the importance of understanding the socio-cultural dimensions of health and disease. Hence most of the studies carried out on tribals have indicated the importance of understanding socio-cultural dimensions of health.

Concept of Health and Disease

The concept of health varies from individual to individual. Generally the tribal groups are guided by their customary traditions. The usual theory of disease in tribal society that it

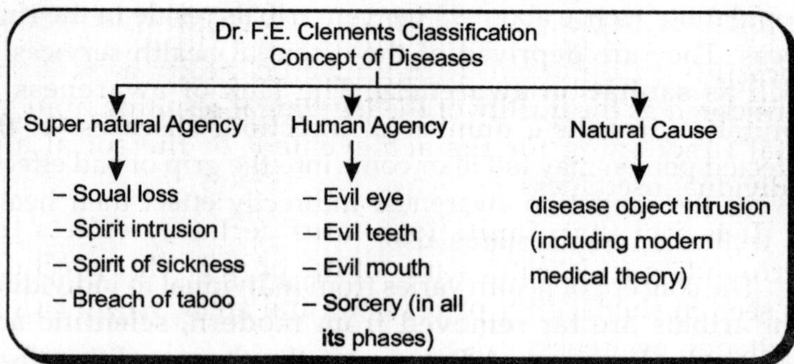

is caused by the breach of some taboo or by hostile spirits, the ghosts or the dead. Sickness is the routine punishment for every lapse and crime meted out to them by the spirits.

Biswas (1934) illustrated primitive[2] concept of disease classification of element and Rivers[3] which may be represented as.

River's Classification

1. Those in which some mobile object or substance is projected into the body of the victim. This is limited to Indonesia, Papuo–Menlaisia and American.
2. Those in which something is abstracted from the body. It is practiced only in India and Africa.
3. Those in which the sorcerer acts on some part of the body of a person or on some object which has been connected with the body at a person in the belief that thereby he can act on the person as a whole.

The modern science do not believe in the above mentioned concepts. According to modern scientific view about the conceptual thought of diseases is that they are caused or spread by small infectious germs/bodies. It may be spread out by environment/wind or by other means. Most of the diseases have been caused due to our negligence of sanitatory habits.

The concept of health has remained elusive and difficult to define. Most of the people see health as the normal condition of the individual, but they do not think much to determine normal from abnormal. In other words, health care can be considered as the quality of the individual resulting from the total functioning for the achievement of the social and individual usefulness.

It is fact that, sanitation status certainly effects the surrounding and health status of the person. This effect can be seen in slums, dirty places and rural areas, where lack of sanitation awareness exists.

Prevalence of Diseases

Poverty compelled with poor standard of hygiene sanitation and nonacceptance of a small and spaced family are responsible for such a high prevalence of anemia in tribal women[4].

A good number of women along with their young children had some problems of illness. A number of cases of pyrexia, diarrhoea, leucorrhea, pain abdomen, otitis, U.T.I. and P.C.M. etc. were seen.[5]

Similarly the prevalence of infection is of the order of about 40 per cent in all age groups rising from about 2 per cent in youngest age group to about 70 per cent at age 35 years. The incidence of infection is highest in individuals between the ages of 5 and 20 years. The risk of infection is of the order of about 2–4 per cent per annum.[6]

Symptoms suggestive of pulmonary Tuberculosis were found in 40 males (10.10%) and 32 females (8.42%) out of 396 males and 380 females.[7] The T.B. is caused due non-awareness and negligence of sanitary habits.

The tribals are addict of liquor and tobacco. Many diseases caused due to their addiction habits. Liquor caused T.B., while tobacco also caused T.B., Cancer and other diseases. In a survey conduction by Dr. Bordia[8] found that 81.10 per cent male were tobacco users, while 18.94 per cent female were tobacco users. He further analyses that 89.49 per cent male were bide smokers, 27.84 per cent male chewed tobacco and 9.65 per cent smoked chilum.

The tobacco caused a number infection on the human body. Dr. Bordia[9] identified that 5.76 per cent men suffered from chronic obstructive lung disease, while 8.06 per cent clinical evidence of acid peptic disease. Tobacco use was present in 100 per cent subjects of obstructive lung disease and 94.28 per cent men with acid peptic disease. Other tobacco hazards which were clinically apparent were poor, oral and dental hygiene and early ageing.

A survey conducted by T.R.I., Rajasthan in Jhadol Panchayat Samiti[10] in the year 1983, found the T.B., Guinea-worm, Asthama, cold and cough, Eye diseases, stomach ache, headache, ear diseases prevalent in the area.

Health Services

The tribals are living in remote areas and scattered habitants, so they have been deprived by the health services. According to 1977 Bench Mark survey[11] conducted by Tribal Research Institute, Rajasthan, Udaipur the position of health services in Tribal Sub–Plan Area are detailed in Table–1.

According to the Bench March survey 1977 only 486 Health Units (Hospital/Dispensaries) were working in the T.S.P. Area, out of 265 were Allopathic, 221 were Ayurvedic. The highest number of the institutions were serving in Udaipur district.

Table 5.1: Availability of Health Services (percentage of Phala/Village)

S.No.	District	Distance from Hospital								
		Less than 1 km	1–2 km	2–3 km	3–5 km	5–10 km	10–15 km	15–20 km	more than 20 km	Total
1.	Udaipur	6.78	13.96	9.69	11.73	25.76	10.43	6.84	7.55	100.00
2.	Chittorgarh	11.42	15.88	14.04	17.06	26.51	8.66	5.25	1.18	100.00
3.	Dungarpur	11.48	29.83	17.17	19.19	15.80	6.53	—	—	100.00
4.	Banswara	7.21	23.04	11.54	20.46	26.68	6.74	1.80	2.53	100.00
5.	Sirohi	7.36	13.42	9.10	16.45	16.45	16.45	4.76	16.10	100.00
	Total	8.71	20.97	13.16	18.08	23.84	8.72	3.72	2.80	100.00

The process of expansion of health services is in progress, but the position of awareness about health is extremely poor. Most of the tribals are ignorant about sanitation status. They are living in very bad environmental situation. Their houses are dirty, so they may become victim of a number of infectious diseases. Most of them do not know about it. Hence there is an urgent need to study their health practices adopted by them, so that they may be provided better environment situation.

Why this Study

According to 1991 census the tribal population of India constitute 67,758,380 persons (34,363,271 male and 33, 395, 109 female) *i.e.* 8.08 per cent of the total pupulation, while in Rajasthan the tribal population constitute 5,474,881 persons (5,837,014 male and 2,637,867 female) *i.e.* 12.44 per cent. The state population is just double of the National Tribal population is just double of the National Tribal population. The total population of Udaipur district consists of 2,89,301 persons (2,395,282 male and 494. 019 female), the tribal population the Udaipur district consists of 1,063,071 persons (1,035,573 rural and 27, 498 Urban) *i.e.* 36.79 per cent of the total district population, which is about three times more than the state tribal population percentage. According to 2001 census the tribal population of India constitute 84,326,240 which constitute 802 per cent population to total population. Similarly 56,50,7185 persons (29420011 male and 27087177 female) reside in the state Rajasthan. Out of which 70,97,706 persons (36,50,982 male and 34,46,724 female) were tribals *i.e.* 12.56 per cent over tribals. The details of S.T. Population is given in chapter–2, Table 2.2. According to Table 2.2 the Udaipur district have 30.71 per cent tribal population, out of which 72.99 per cent Rural and 10.61 per cent Urban population.

The tribals live in remote places and in dense forests also. The tribals are economically very backward and they are cut-off from the civilized world. They are too much backward, so the government of India listed them in schedule for special privilege in constitution.

The concept of health varies from individual to individual. Most of the people see health as the normal condition of the individual. Some see health as opposite of illness, disease of sickness. In other words, health can be considered as the quality of individual resulting from the total functioning for the achievement of the social and individual usefulness.

In fact, the sanitation status certainly effects the surrounding and the health status of the person. This effect can be seen easily in rural areas, where lack of sanitation awareness exists.

Universe

This study was conducted in the Tribal Sub Plan Area of the state Rajasthan. For this purpose one district *i.e.* Udaipur district, which have all the tribal groups along with different economic status are residing has been selected for the study. Out of ten tehsils *viz.* Girwa, Sarada, Salumber, Kerwara, Dariyawad, Jhadol, Kotra, Mavli, Gogunda and Vallabhnagar, Seven tehsiles have tribal concentration *i.e.* Girva, Sarada, Salumber, Kherwara, Dhariyawad, Jhodol and Kotra. The present form of district came into existence from April 11, 1991.

Out of the 7 tribal concentrated Panchayat samities, two of them have been selected for the study. Girwa and Jhadol have been selected for the study, because Girwa is nearer to urban area and Jhadol is remote. Hence it is assumed that the tribals residing in Girwa Panchayat Samiti may have more awarness, while - Jhadol is remote one. From each Panchayat Samiti 2 villages have been selected for the study, first is nearer to the Panchayat Samiti head quarter, while second is remote. Hence by this way from Girwa Panchayat Samiti (1) Dhol-Ki-pati, (2) Chhoti Undri and from Jhadol Panchayat Samiti (1) Shayampura, (2) Malpur have been selected for the field work.

From each village 25 per cent persons would be selected by simple random sampling method, but maximum 15 persons *i.e.* male/female from each village have been selected. Hence 60 persons have been selected for the study. For this purpose beneficiaries and official schedules have been introduced.

REFERENCES

1. Census of India, 1991, Series – 1, paper I of 1993, Union Primary Census Abstract for S.C. and S.T. pp. 44–57
2. Buddhadeb Chudhuri (Ed.): *Tribal Health Socio–Cultural Dimensions*, Inter-India publication (1986), p. 162.
3. *Ibid*, p, 162.
4. Dr. H.N. Mathur: *Anaemia in Tribal Women, Survey and Management* (1988), Sponsored by T.R.I. (Raj.), Udaipur, p. 25.
5. *Ibid*, p. 32.
6. Dr. H.N. Mathur: *Detection and Management of Pulmonary Tuberculosis is Tribal Population (1990),* sponsored by. T.R.I. (Raj.), Udaipur. p. 4
7. *Ibid*, p. 14.
8. Dr. Arun Bordia: Survey of Tobacco Smoking and Chewing in Tribal Area of Udaipur: *Psychosocial Aspects, Economic impact and Health Implication* 1991, Sponsored by T.R.I. Raj, Udaipur. p. 7–8
9. *Ibid*, pp. 23–25
10. *Health Coverage: A study of Jhadol Panchayat Samiti* (1983), T.R.I., Rajasthan Udaipur. p. 14
11. Mehta, Prakash Chandra: *Tribal Health and Medical Services–An Analysis*. Tribe Vol. 25, No. 1–2 March–June T.R.I., Rajasthan, Udaipur. p. 14–15

6 Personal Hygiene

The environmental factors considerably affect the health of the community as a whole. Personal hygiene, affects primarily the health of individual and is by and large connected with standard of living. It requires awareness of the individual's particular habits which grow by practice and eventually became part of their culture.

Most of the studies made on tribal communities have indicated the importance of understanding the socio–cultural dimensions of health and diseases. A number of deities are often associated with disease or diseases is connected with the interference of supernatural agency and naturally the nature of treatment in such cases is also made accordingly. In fact, there is an urgent need to understand and identify the cause of illness as the nature of treatment is intimately connected with the cause identified.

In this chapter I have discussed the essential components for a healthy person which are very necessary for hygiene that makes a man healthy and free from infectious and diseases due to awareness and healthy environment.

ABLUTION PRACTICES

Defection Habit

They usually get-up very early in the morning and go to field for defection. Usually they carry a lota (made of brass or tumbler made of tin) of water and wash the parts after defection. They usually go for defection in early morning every day, if necessary they go for defection at any time of the day or night in the nearby field or any convenient open place. They wash their hands after defection by Soil/Ash/Soap whichever is easily available. They generally use soil for washing hands, because it is easily available every where. They also use ash for washing hands which is also easily available. If soap is available they do not hesitate to wash their hands with it.

It is notable that in the rainy days they do not carry lota, they sit near the stream of water or pond and wash the parts with pond water/stream water after defection. They do not use latrines.

The village-wise habit of defection, washing of hands, mode of washing and washing of lota have been discussed in Table 6.1.

The Table 6.1 reveals that cent percent tribals having habit of defection in early morning and wash their hands after defection. Generally they wash their hands with soil (mud).

Cleaning of Mouth, Teeth and Throat

After coming back from the defection, generally they wash their mouth and face and clean their teeth. In rainy days they was their mouth, teeth and throat at the same place of stream water/pond water where they have washed their parts and hands after defection. Such type of washing is most unhygienic for health, but they do not know the hazards of it. This habit is responsible for carrying infection and re-infection of gastro-intestinal and water born diseases.

They wash their teeth with rubbing their finger on it, several times they use ash to clean their teeth. Casually they use *Neem* or *Babul* stick (*datun*) to clean their teeth. They do not use tooth paste or any kind of tooth powder. Cent percent respondents are cleaning their mouth, teeth and throat with water. This type of washing is not enough for healthy teeth. It may cause many infectious diseases.

Table 6.1: Village-wise Habit of Defection

(Number)

Sl. No.	Name of village	Habit of Daily		Washing of lands after					Washing of lota defections defection	
						Mode of washing				
		Yes	No.	Yes	No	Soil	Ash	Soap	Yes	No
1	Dhol–Ki–Pati	15	–	15	–	15	10	5	15	–
2	Chhoti Undri	15	–	15	–	15	1	13	–	15
3	Shyampura	15	–	15	–	15	10	4	15	–
4	Malpur	15	–	15	–	15	6	12	2	13
	Total	60	–	60	–	60	27	34	32	28

Table 6.2: Village-wise Bathing Habit of Respondents

(Number)

Sl. No.	Name of Village	Bathing				Bathing of family members daily		Females bath daily during menstruation	
		Yes	No	Daily	Alter-nate day	Yes	No	Yes	No
1	Dhol–Ki–Pati	15	–	14	1	14	1	3	12
2	Chhoti Undri	15	–	7	8	8	7	6	9
3	Shyampura	15	–	15	–	9	6	4	11
4	Malpur	15	–	6	9	8	7	5	10
	Total	60	–	42	18	39	21	18	42

Bathing Habits

Case of the skin is largely related with the bathing habit of the individual. There are two common sources of water in the village. Village well and village ponds. Now a days handpumps are also popular among them.

The tribals understand in bathing, but they do not take their bath in early morning. They take their bath when they feel free. Generally they do not use soap for bathing, because they can not afford. The village-wise details of their bathing habit is given in Table 6.2.

Clothing

Clothing is an essential social need for the man. From the biological point of view clothes sustain the warmth of the body and protect it against heat and cold along with from external injuries. As a social need clothing are necessary for decency and personal decoration.

In ancient time tribals used only very essential clothes to cover their body, but with passing time they have started use of more clothes. Now a days they are wearing all the essential clothes as other persons wear.

The habit of washing clothes in the tribals can be seen regular. Generally they do not change their clothes daily, but most of them changed their dress alternate day. Generally they rins their clothes in water and dry up in sunlight. This is their general mode of washing clothes. This practice is adopted by male and female both. They casually use soap for washing their economic constraints. The village-wise changing habit of clothing is detailed in Table 6.3.

Table 6.3: Village-wise Habit of Changing Clothes

(Number)

Sl. No.	Name of Village	Changing of cloth		
		Daily	Alternate day	More than three days
1	Dhol-Ki-Pati	3	12	–
2	Chhoti Undri	–	15	–
3	Shyampura	2	11	2
4	Malpur	–	15	
	Total	5	53	2

The Table 6.3 reveals that out of 60 respondents, 5 (8.33%) changing their clothes daily, 53 (88.33%) alternate day and rest 2 (3.34%) were changing their clothes more than three day. This type of practice is unhygienic.

Cleanness of House

The housing pattern in the tribal society is much different as compared to non-tribal. They have their scattered houses on the hills and rocks. Generally they do not like to reside in the plane area. The built their huts in between or near by their field. On the name of house, triabls have only a single room (hut) which is constructed by local material like stones, mud and grass, etc. They thatch their hut by bamboos and earthen tiles. Hence in the name of different rooms they have only a multipurpose cottage which serves them kitchen, bedroom, store, etc. They do not put any sort of ventilation in their hut and have only single door for entrance. In rainy days and in night they also tie their goats and hens in their hut. Overall the environment of hut can not be said hygienic.

They use wood or dry cow dung for cooking their food. While cooking, their is no exit of smoke, hence during cooking hours the atmosphere of the hut becomes most unhygienic. Over all they do not care about the cleanness of their hut. Casually they coat their hut with the mixture of mud and cow dung, this process is locally known as lipai. The atmosphere of the huts of the tribals can be said unhygienic. The environment of huts surely affect the health of the residing persons. Another feature of their house is that they do not care about the cleanness of their sublings.

They brush their hut by the palm brush or grass brush. They also clean their animals court yard. They only brush their huts, but they do not care the hygienic atmosphere of their hut. The village-wise details of cleaning their huts are detailed in Table 6.4.

Table 6.4: Village-wise Cleaning Habit

(Number)

Sl. No.	Name of village	Cleaning of house daily		Cleaning of animal court yard	
		Yes	No	Yes	No
1	Dhol–Ki–Pati	15	–	15	–
2	Chhoti Undri	13	2	15	–
3	Shyampura	15	–	15	–
4	Malpur	15	–	11	4
	Total	58	2	56	4

The Table 6.4 reveals that out 60 respondify 58 (96.67%) brush their houses daily, while 23 (33%) brush their houses in alternate day. Cent percent respondents brush their animal court yard daily.

Generally the tribals tie up their animals nearby their house. They try to keep their animals neat and clean, but due to their negligence and business they do not pay more attention towards this side. The village-wise details of animals cleaning habit is given in Table 6.5.

Table 6.5: Village-wise Cleaning of Animals

(Number)

Sl. No.	Name of Village	Cleaning of animals	
		Yes	No.
1.	Dhol-Ki–Pati	11	4
2.	Chhoti Undri	15	–
3.	Shyampura	9	6
4.	Malpur	1	14
	Total	36	24

Out of 60 respondents, 36 (60%) clean their animals daily, while 24 (40%) do clean their animals in regular manner.

Daily Habits

Daily habits means the essential precautions which are necessary for point of hygiene have been strictly observed are covered in this clause.

Washing of hands before taking meals protect any person from many infections caused by small germs, similarly covering of edibles are protected from infections as-well-as approach of unhygienic particles. Regular care of patient is essential for early recovery. Similarly filtered water protects the person from many infections as-well-as from water born diseases. The village-wise details of their habit are given in Table 6.6.

The Table 6.6 revels that out of 60 repondents, 23 (38.33%) wash their hands before taking meals, while rest 37 (61.67%) do not care about this.

Out of 60 respondents, 47 (78.33%) were covering the edibles, while, 13 (21.67) do not pay any attention regarding covering the food material. The reason behind this is that they are careless about this practice and do not know the hazards of non-covering.

Out of 60 respondents, 36 (60%) tribals atend their patients regularly, while 24 (40%) do not pay much attention about the patients of family.

The tribals do not pay required attention towards the diet of the patient. Out of 60 respondences 8(13.33%) reported regarding special diet for the patient. This is due to their poor economic condition by which they are not in a position to afford special diet of the patient.

Out of 60 respondents, 37(61.67%) tribals pay special attention towards the patient regarding sanitation and rest 23(38.33%) do not pay much attention. But during the field survey it has been observed that tribal persons do not know more about the sanitation practices required to be adopted during the illness period. They only take precautions whatever they know. Such type of behaviour is not enough for the hygiene.

Out of 60 respondents, 19 (31.67%) filter the dotable water, while rest 41 (68.33%) do not bother about filtration of water.

Table 6.6: Village-wise Daily Habit

(Number)

Sl. No.	Name of Village	Washing hands before taking		Covering the etables		Regular care of patient		Special food to given to the patient		Special care of patient and their sanitation		Regular filter of potable water	
		Yes	No	Yes	No	Yes	No	Yes	No	Yes	No	Yes	No
1	Dhol-ki-Pati	4	11	12	3	12	3	4	11	14	1	7	8
2	Chhoto-Undir	2	13	13	2	5	10	–	15	8	7	2	
3	Shyampura	3	12	15	5	10	5	4	11	10	5	4	11
4	Malpur	14	1	12	3	9	6	–	15	5	10	6	9
	Total	23	37	47	13	36	24	8	52	37	23	19	41

Swatch have given funnel and clothes free of cost to the tribals and get acquainted with the hazards of unfiltered use of water, but after damage of mesh of funnel or torn of cloth they do not use such type of device. It has been observed that tribals do not want to spend a single paney on such device. Hence they generally use unfiltered potable water. Their water pots are not clean, because they do not pay proper attention towards cleaning the pots regularly.

Prevailing Diseases

The prevailing common diseases in the area of cold, cough, fever, malaria, diarrhoea, leucorrhoea, pain abdomen, otitis, T.B., skin diseases and general diseases like syphilis, Gonorrhoea, chancroid, etc. V.D. is a genetic germ which includes a number of sexual diseases caused due to infection carried during intercourse *i.e.* sexually transmitted disease.

For general diseases both the medical and social factors play their significant role in the context.

The tribals are not aware about the diseases and are not in a position to afford costly treatment. Generally they take treatment of a local priest known as *Bhopa*. They also use local herbs for their treatment which are readily available to them without any cost or at a nominal price. Generally they try to avoid allopathic treatment. If such type of treatment is available at their village free of cost, they take allopathic treatment. Most of the respondents have been found taking their treatment from *Bhopa* or any other local means. In severe condition they go for treatment in the nearby city, but it has been observed in very rare cases of critical condition, because they can not afford such type of very costly treatment due to their economic constraints.

The tribals immunise their siblings where the medical facilities/health centres are available by motivation of health workers/nursing staff, but the tribals of the remote villages do not care about the immunisation/vaccination. The village wise details of immunisation/vaccination are detailed in Table 6.7.

Table 6.7: Village-wise Immunisation/Vaccination

(Number)

Sl. No.	Name of village	Immunisation/ vaccination		If 'Yes' Regular	
		Yes	No.	Yes	No.
1	Dhol-Ki-Pati	15	–	15	
2	Chhoti Undri	6	9	6	–
3	Shyampura	15	–	15	–
4	Malpur	14	1	15	–
	Total	50	10	51	–

The Table 6.7 reveals that out of 60 respendents, 50 (83.33%) tribal families were immunised/vaccinate their sublings, while rest 10 (16.67%) do not pay attention toward this side.

Awarness about Sanitation

Most of the tribals know that dirtyness causes diseases but they do not take it seriously. They take it easily and do not pay proper attention towards the cleanness of their surrounding as-well-as cleanness of body. Due to their

Table 6.8: Village-wise Awareness

(Number)

Sl.No	Name of the village	Sanitation awareness		Transmission of sanitation awareness		Knowledge about the benefits of sanitation		Knowledge of sanitation of your family members	
		Yes	No.	Yes	No	Yes	No.	Yes	No
1	Dhol-Ki-Pati	15	–	6	9	15	–	14	1
2	Chhoti Undri	14	1	14	–	13	2	4	11
3	Shyampura	15	–	12	3	14	1	13	2
4	Malpur	15	–	1	14	12	3	13	2
	Total	59	1	33	26	54	6	44	16

negligence and traditional social environment they do not want to obey or observe the new healthy modes which are very essential for the health. The illiteracy is also a hurdle in the way. Seva Mandir is extending health and awareness services in tribal blocks of Udaipur district through a number of para workers, but the govt. is not taking pains in this matter. Perhaps I.E.C. Bureau is extending there services regarding family planning and immunisation/vaccination.

The village-wise details of awareness and their transmission is given in Table 6.8.

Addition Habit

Addiction of any sort of intoxicant is hazardxus for the health. It may caused a number of infections and due to this a person may come into the grip of many diseases. The tribals are generally addict of liquor, because they extract liquor in their own way at their own homes. Hence they do not spent any thing on liquor. In tribal society male and female both enjoy liquor. Their social customs are incomplete without liquor. During the festivals they use liquor in planty and fully enjoy the festivals like Holi and Diwali. The tribals also use Ganja and often use tobacco in the form of bidi and chewing it.

The village-wise details of their addiction habit is given in Table 6.9.

Table 6.9:Village-wise Addiction Habit

(Number)

Sl. No.	Name of village	Use of intoxicants		Knowledge about the hazards of intoxication	
		Yes	No.	Yes	No.
1.	Dhol-Ki-Pati	9	6	15	–
2.	Chhoti Undri	11	4	15	–
3.	Shyampura	8	7	9	6
4.	Malpur	12	3	12	3
	Total	40	20	51	9

Table 6.9 reveals that out of 60 respondents, 40(67.37%) are addict and rest 20(33.33) causally use intoxicants. They generally use local made liquor and smoke bidi, liquor and bidi are used by male and females both.

Hence the tribals have little knowledge about the personal hygiene, and do not have enough knowledge about the environmental hazards and infections caused due to their dirty and other modes. The present machinery engaged by the government in the health services is not enough for creating the awareness through programmes undertaken by them about the hygiene.

Bibliography

1. Aarens, A. and Hugh Howes, (1979), *Child to Child,* MacMillan, London.
2. Advani, Mohan (1967), *Social Science Studies on Health in India,* A Brief Bibliographical Analysis passes in the Conference on Review of Behavioural Research in Health Extension Eduction, Central Health Eduction Bureau, New Delhi.
3. Ahmed, S.L. (1975) : "*A Study of Child Rearing Practice Among the Adivasi and Harijans of Chottanagpur.*" Bulletin of A.S.I., 24 (1 and 2), 17–20.
4. American Academy of readings (1943), Recommended Standards for the Operation of mothers milk bureaux." J. Pediat, 23, 112.
5. Aurora, G.S. (1969), "*Towards a Sociology of Food and Nutrition of India.*" Social action, 19(2), 1–2.
6. Bahadur, K.P. (1978), *Caste, Tribe and Culture of India,* Vol. IV Karnataka, Keral and Tamil Nadu. EssEss Publications. New Delhi.
7. Bahadur, K.P. (1978), *Caste, Tribes and Culture of India,* Vol. V, EssEss Publication, New Delhi.
8. Bildhaiya, B. and Pemeld, C. (1968) – "A Study of Some Present Customs and Beliefs for the Health and Well-beings of Children." *Indian Journal of Public Health,* 12(4), 215–218.
9. Black-fan K.D. Ed. (1933), *Growth and Development of Child. Part–I Anatomy and Physiology.* White Conference Child Health and Protection, New York and London.
10. Bogert, L.J. (1960), *Nutrition and Physical Fitness,* W.B Sanders Company. Philadelphia.

11. Bouslog. J.S. Gunningham. T.D. Hanner, J.P. and Waltz, H.D. (1935), *Roentgenologic Studies of the Infants Gastroinestial Tract,* J. Pendit. 6,234.

12. Breckenridge, Marine E. and Vincent E. Lee, *Child Development : Physical and Psychological Growth through Adolexence* (Vth Edition), W.B. Saunders Company, philadelphia and London.

13. British Medical Association (1950); Report of the Committee on Nutrition, London.

14. Burgess, A. and Dean, R.F.A. (Ed.) 1962; *Malnutrition and Food Habits."* Tavistock Publications London.

15. Bay-lay, N. (1969); Bayley Scales of Infant Development, Psychological Corporation, New York.

16. Carstirs, G.M. (1955); *Medicine and Faith in rural Rajasthan, in Health, Culture and Community* (Ed.) B.D. Paul, russel sage function, New York.

17. Chaudhuri, Buddhadey (Ed.); *Tribal Health; sociocultural Dimensions,* Inter-India publications, New Delhi.

18. Choudhury, N.C. (1977); *Munda Social Structure,* Firmak L.M Private Limited, Calculate.

19. Clements, F.W. (1949); *Infants Nutrition; Its Physiological Basis.* Bristol.

20. Census of India, 1961, 1971 and 1981 : *Social and Cultural Tables and Special Tables of Scheduled Tribes.*

21. Census of India, 1961, 1971, 1981, 1991 and 2001 General Population tables.

22. Census of India, Series-18, *Rajasthan, District census Handbook,* Udaipur district.

23. Devision, Sir S. and Passmore, R (1963); *Human Nutrition and Dieties.* 2nd Edimburg and London.

24. Davise. C. (1928); Self-selection of diet by Newly Weaned Infants; Amer J. Dis. child 36,651.

25. Desouja, Alfred (Ed.) 1979; *Children in India,* Manohar New Delhi.

26. Dinkmeyer, D.C. 1967; *Child Development.*

27. Doshi, J.K.; *Social Structure and Cultural Change in a Bhil village,* New Heights, Delhi.

28. Doshi. S.L. (1978); *Between Societal Self-awareness and Cultural Synthesis.*

29. Dutta, P.C. (1955); *Rural Health and Medical Care in India* Army Educational Press, Ambala.

30. Elestad - Sayed. J. (1979); *Breast Feeding Protects against Infection in India Infants,* Canadian Medical Association Journal, 20 : 295–293.

31. Elliott D. Landau, Epstein, Sherrice Landau and stone, Ann planat (Edu.); *Child Development through Literature.* Prentice-Hall, Inc. Englewood Cliffs, New-Jersey.

32. Ellis, Richarel W.B. (Ed. 1966); *Child Health and Development* (IVth Edition), J & A Churchill Ltd, London.

33. Evans, P. and Mackeith, R. (1954); *Infant Feeding and Feeding Difficulties* (3rd Edn.) London.

34. Elwin, V. (1953); *A Great Tribal Medicine-man,* Statesman, March 29.

35. Elwin, V. (1943); *Conception, Pregnancy and Birth among the Tribesman of Mikir Hills,* Journal of the Royal Asiatic society Press (India Branch), Delhi.

36. Forbes, G.B. (1957); *Over-nutrition of the Child : Blessing or Curse?* Nutrict review 15, 193.

37. Future; A Quaterly Journal of UNICEF. 2 to 27.

38. Gosh, Shanti (1977); *The Feeding and Care of Infants and Young Children.* Voluntary Health Association of India, New Delhi.

39. Gopalan, C. (1971); *Diet Atlas of India, National Institute of Nutrition,* Hyderabad.

40. Gwatkin, Davidson, R. (1974) ; *Health and Nutrition in India,* (Mimeograph), Ford Foundation, New Delhi.

41. Hurlock, Elizabeth; *Child Development.*

42. Iliingworth, R.S. (1953); *Abnormal Substances Excreted in Human Milk,* Practitioner, 171, 533.

43. Jeans, P.C. and Marriott, W.M. (1974); *Infant Nutrition* (4th Edt.), London.

45. Kappuswami, B. (1976); *Bal Vyavahar Aurvikas,* Vikas Publishing House, Delhi.

46. Kaur, Surjit (1978); *Wastage of Children*, Sterling Publishers, New Delhi.

47. Kon, S.K. and Mawson, E.H. (1950); Human Milk, M.R.C. Special Report Ser. No. 269. H.M.S.O. Lewis P. Ldpsitt and Charles C. Spiker; Advances in *Child Development and behaviour* (Val. I)

48. Mackay, H.M.S. (1939); *Vitamin A Requirements of Children*, Arch, Dis. Childh. 14,254.

49. Mahadevan, Indira (1962); *Social Factors in some Nutritional Deficiency Diseases*, Indian Journal of Social Work, 23 : 41–52.

50. Mathux, Dr. H.N. (1990); *Detection and Management of Pulmonary Tuberculosis in Tribal Population*, project sponsored by T.R.I., Rajasthan, Udaipur.

51. May, C.D. (1959); Determination and significance of a dietary allowance of Protein for Infants Pediatrics. 23, 384.

52. Mead, Margaret (1962); Coming of Age in Samoa.

53. Mieler, R.A. (1952); *Factors Influencing Location*. I–Material, II–Pre. Maturity and Abnormal Labour, III–Abnormaltities of breast. Arch, Dis. Child, 27. 187, 195,200.

54. Murdok, Georgepeter; Our Primitive Contemporaries.

55. Mussen, Paul, Henery Conger, John. Janeway and Kadgan Jerome (Eds.); *Readings, in Child Development and Personality*, Harper and Row Publishers, New York, Evaniton and London.

56. Naish, F.C. (1956); *Breast feeding*, 2nd Edn.; Lloydluke Ltd, London.

57. National Institute of Public Cooperation and Child Development (1976); the Study of the Young Child : Indian case study Nipcod, New Delhi.

58. Pai, D.N. and Eutructur, M.I. (1964) : *Health of Rural Adivasis in India*–Journal of Medical sciences, 18(3), 716.

59. Paul. B.D. (Ed.) 1955; *Health, Culture and Community* Russel Sage Foundation, New York.

60. Pratap. D.R. and Rao, V.V.R. 1972; The Nutritional Status of the Pre-school children, pregnant and lactating mothers among the chenchus (Mimeographed); Tribal Cultural Research and Training Institute, Hyderabad, A.P.

61. Raj. S. Mobinddin; *The Process of Socialization* : A Multi-Ethnic Study, Chetana Publications, New Delhi.

62. Ram Kumar; *Women Health Development and Administration*: Principles and Practices Val I & II, Deep and Deep Publications, New Delhi.

63. Ratcliff, T.A. 1970; *The Child and Reality,* George Allen and Unwin Limited, London.

64. Raza, Moonis and Nangia, Sudesh 1986, *Atlas of the Child in India,* Concept Publishing Company, New Delhi.

65. Ruhela, Satya Pal (1984); *The children of Indian Nomades,* Sterling Publishing Private Ltd., New Delhi.

66. Mussen. Paul H. Conger, Hohn J. and Kagan, Jerome (1974); *Child Development and Personality* (4th edition) Harper and row publishers, New York, Evanston, San Fransis.

67. Scammon, R.E. 1923; *A Summary of the Anatomy of the Infant and Child* in Pediatrics ed. A. Abt. I, 257. Philadelphia.

68. Sharma, Krishna; The Konds of Orissa An Anthopometric Study.

69. Smith, C.A. 1959; *The Physiology of the Newborn Infant.* 3rd edn. Oxford.

70. Smith, C.A. (1962); *Prenatal and Neonatal Nutrition* Pediatrics. 30, 145.

71. Srinivasan, K. Saxena, P.C. Kabitkar Tara (Eds.) 1979 ; *Demographic and Socio-economic Aspects of Child in India.* Himalays Publishing House, Bombay.

72. Stuart and Prugh 1973; *The Healthy Child : His Physical Psychological and Social Development,* Harvard University press (sixth Printing) London.

73. Sukhatme, P.V.; Malnutrition and Poverty, Ninth Lal Bahadur Shastri Memorial Lecture, Indian Agricultural Research Institute, London.

74. Symposium 1947; Lacation : Function and Product. British Medical Bulletin, 5, 1099.

75. Swaminathan, Mina; The Pre-school Child in India: Assignment children, 21. Jan–Mar. 1973, 3–18.

76. Sweemer, Cecilede Sengupta, Nandita K. and Sheila B. Takulia (Eds.) 1978 ; *Manual for Child Nutrition in Rural India;* Voluntary Health Association of India. New Delhi.

77. Taylor, R. (1917); *Hunger in the Infant*; Amer J.Ds. Child, 14, 233.

78. Tyson R.M. Shradar E.A. and Perlman H.H.(1937–1938); *Drugs Transmitted Through Breast Bilk*. J. Pendiat, II 824, 13,86,91.

79. UNICEF (1964); *Children of the Developing Countries* (A Report) Thomas Nelson and Sons Ltd., London.

80. Vidyarthi, L.P. and Rai; *The Tribal Culture of India.*

81. Walter, James and Nick Stinnett; Parent-Child Relationship; A Decade Review of Research, In Journal of Marriage and Family, 33, N–1 February 1971, 70–111.

82. Whiting, Beatric B; Six Cultures : Studies of Child Rearing.

83. Wickes. I.G. (1953); *A History of Infant Feeding Arch.* Dis. Childh. 28,159,232, 332, 416, 495.

84. Wolf, O.H.(1955); *Obesity and Childhood,* A Study of the Birth Weight, Height and the Onest of Puperty, Quart. J.Med. 24, 109.

85. Ziemska, Maria (1978), Early Child Care in Ploand, Gordon and Breach, London.

Index

J

K

M

N

P

R

S

T

U

W